Marilyn's Story

The cases I reveal in my books are all based on true experiences, but I have changed names and some details to protect their identities as they go on to build new lives and families of their own.

THROWN AWAY **CHILDREN**

Marilyn's Story

Louise Allen

with Theresa McEvoy

MIRROR BOOKS

m
B

MIRROR BOOKS

1

Published in Great Britain and Ireland in 2024 by
Mirror Books, a Reach PLC business,
5 St Paul's Square, Liverpool, L3 9SJ.

www.mirrorbooks.co.uk
@TheMirrorBooks

Print ISBN 9781915306630
eBook ISBN 9781915306647

Design and production by Mirror Books.

Printed and bound in Great Britain by
CPI Group (UK) Ltd, Croydon, CR0 4YY

Cover image: Adobe Stock
(Posed by model)

This book was printed using
FSC approved materials.

MIX
Paper | Supporting
responsible forestry
FSC
www.fsc.org   FSC® C171272

Contents

Foreword

In telling *Marilyn's Story*, I'm attempting to weave together a narrative surrounding a child who was in my care for a relatively short space of time. Inevitably, therefore, I don't have all the details about her life before or after her time with me. Much is pieced together from what she told me. Marilyn's story is linked to a wider story of County Lines: the use of children and vulnerable people by organised criminal gangs to distribute drugs from the big cities into smaller towns ans rural areas.

Sadly, Marilyn's story is not the first time I've encountered this frightening phenomenon. It's a strange phrase, 'county lines', with overtones of the Wild West and sheriffs with no jurisdiction beyond their county boundaries.

In reality, 'county lines' refers to mean the one telephone line used to order illegal drugs, and shared often using social media, business cards, or even printed on the sides of giveaway cigarette lighters. The influence of County Lines is nationwide. While cannabis has been widely linked to the County Lines organisations, it is harder drugs that provide the focus: heroin, cocaine and amphetamines. The County Lines gangs use standard business techniques to develop their trade. In a new area, they need to offer discounts, a consistent quality product, and make sure it is reliably delivered. That's where the children come in: street gangs, ultimately managed by shadowy organised crime gangs, are the hub of County Line activity and are forced to 'go country', to distribute and deliver the drugs.

Grooming takes place at a surprisingly young age, and the victims are always young people who want the kudos of being part of the gang and its allure of ready cash, clothes, cars and respect. Others close to the gang members: their families, friends and neighbours – reluctant affiliates – are drawn into the gang's sphere of influence too, as is the case in *Marilyn's Story*.

Since part of Marilyn's story took place while she was in my care, I'm also telling a story of my own experience as a foster carer and the reality of what being a foster carer means. If you have read my other books you already know that I say it 'as it is'. I have no concern about whether the social workers or their superiors like me or not. Indeed, I suspect the latter may be true more often than not.

Where do stories start? Marilyn's story is heartbreaking, but it doesn't begin with the moment of her birth. What happened to her has its roots in a story that starts much further back, I think. Maybe with her mother, Emily. Or perhaps it begins even further back, with Marilyn's grandparents, Rebecca and Robert's story.

Our own story is never entirely our own. Individual stories are entwined in the lives of others. Who knows where each begins and ends?

PART ONE

Emily

I

Before

'Here will do.'

Rebecca stops and indicates an area of pavement just ahead of them.

About time, thinks Emily, who has broken into a sweat with the effort it has taken to push her cart up the steep hill from their home.

The spot that her mother has chosen for today's 'public witnessing' is just along from the Co-op shop, next to some railings. Weeds have broken through the concrete paving.

Sylvia is behind. She waits for Emily to manoeuvre her customised sack truck into position and then slides hers next to Emily's. They begin to set up, arranging the leaflets and religious tracts so that they can be easily seen by any customers exiting the shop as well as by passers by on the High Street. Rebecca checks the time on her watch and makes a note of it in a little book. 'For the field service report.'

Side by side, the converted barrows look like library shelving on trolley wheels, which is more or less what they are; constructed by Sylvia and Rebecca a few months ago in a move towards supporting their community's decision to branch out into town-centre evangelism. Though they're unwieldy when being pushed uphill, it's worth it. A big improvement on knocking on doors, as far as Emily is concerned.

The downside is that setting up stall like this in town makes them very visible to everyone, including the three Year 11 students that Emily recognises from school who have chosen this moment to appear at the other end of the High Street. Emily knows that standing in front of three shelves full of *The Watchtower* and *Awake!* isn't going to disguise what they're doing here.

As the group moves closer, Emily feels more and more self-conscious. She knows how different she looks from most of her peers. School uniform is a good leveller, but out of school, hours of standing on pavements have given her plenty of time to study what her peers wear. She loves their clothes and the way they do their hair and make-up. She is desperate to wear interesting and fashionable clothes herself, but her mother is set on making everything they wear from rolls of fabric she buys. Emily smooths down her skirt, which is long and flowery, like her mum's and Sylvia's, all cut in the same style: drab and unfashionable. Perhaps they'll go into the shop without seeing her. Her mouth goes dry.

No such luck.

The students giggle and point and Emily knows that they are talking about her. She already has a reputation for being weird at school and this is only going to make things much, much worse. It's so unfair. She doesn't even believe in all this stuff anymore. She only does it because she knows what it would mean to her mum if she were to openly question the faith she is no longer sure about.

Emily feels the heat rush to her neck and knows that the colour has risen to her face. The top of her forehead underneath her neat fringe begins to feel hot and wet.

The girls go into the shop, so there are a few seconds of blessed relief. But soon they are out again, carrying snacks and fizzy drinks.

'Loser,' one mutters. Emily knows it is directed at her, even though the girl doesn't look at her.

Her mother rests a hand on Emily's shoulder. 'Ignore them. Be strong. They are anti-God and doomed to destruction. You are a good girl. Do not be worried by them.'

6

The platitudes from her mother no longer offer the comfort that they once did. Instead they make her feel uneasy. This life no longer feels right. She wonders if it ever did, really.

Because they were not always Jehovah's Witnesses.

Emily loves her mother but remembers her from the time 'before', when she was fun and wore fashionable clothes and mixed with other mums from the school. She misses that version of her mum. Seeing her submissive, sallow, unmade-up face everyday is disturbing. Her mum's hair has become grey and dry. She looks like an old woman. Worse than that, a 'nothing' woman.

Emily blinks back the tears that threaten to come, clamping her teeth together as though the willpower to stop the flood lies in her jaw. She wants to shout out at the top of her voice, 'But this is not who I am!'

These same girls who now mock her and keep away from her at secondary school were once her friends. She used to have birthdays and celebrate Christmas. But her seventh birthday was the last time she had what she now thought of as a 'normal' celebration with birthday cake and presents and a party. It wasn't long after that party that the Jehovah's Witnesses knocked at their door. Her dad was home alone when he answered it. He wouldn't even have been at home if he hadn't been made redundant from the local engineering firm, one of several local businesses that had closed down.

She remembers her dad picking her up from school that day. He was happy for once. He hadn't been happy for a while, not since he lost his job. He told Emily and her mum that life was going to get better: they were going to church and he had been offered some work with a local building firm. He was going to bring in the money again and devote time to showing his love to Jehovah, who had saved them.

That was the turning point. And of course, she had gone along with everything her father had suggested. The whole family was transformed. Her mother's role was to smile and worship her dad, who quickly rose in the hierarchy of the religious community. And now this is her 'normal'. Except, when she sees other teenagers, especially girls, she feels it is anything but normal.

'Nutter,' says the girl in the middle of the group, with a sneer.

They turn and walk back in the direction they came from, back towards the centre of town.

Emily sighs. It could have been much, much worse. Relief washes over her – the ordeal is over. For now. Those girls may have turned away, but she knows it isn't *really* over. She feels a constant tension between conforming and resisting. As time goes on, the ideas that had once been explained to her so simply as a younger child no longer sit comfortably with the ideologies she encounters in secondary school.

It was in an art class last year that she'd had her first real epiphany. Art has always been Emily's favourite subject, but at home her natural creative streak is stifled, reduced these days to knitting and sewing. At school, they'd been learning about different artistic movements for GCSE and a section on Pop Art had appeared on a slide in her teacher's Powerpoint presentation. Emily was immediately drawn to the cleverly subversive nature of the movement. The teacher talked about this artist called Andy Warhol who ate a can of Campbell's soup every day for lunch. He had a big art studio called The Factory in New York.

There were musicians and models and actors all hanging out in this place. Emily was captivated – perhaps in the same way as her father had been on the day of his conversion when the Jehovah's Witnesses knocked on their door. Emily had felt her own awakening, but it was an artistic rather than a spiritual one. There were screen prints of Hollywood actresses Elizabeth Taylor and Marilyn Monroe. Emily was sold. She was going to find a way out of the Jehovah's Witnesses and into art, glamour and fashion. She was not a loser, however much she might be judged by her peers for lifestyle choices that her parents had made for her.

Emily has a sudden longing to follow the girls, even though they've been mean to her, to just be ordinary for a moment. Hang out with people her own age. They're heading in the direction of the town centre.

She spends the next 10 minutes talking to an elderly gentleman in a grey anorak who is too polite to make his escape. Not only does she successfully swerve his conversation-stoppers, she manages to engage him in some dialogue by asking his opinion about the state of things. She uses all the techniques she's been taught to steer the conversation around to theological matters, and manages to persuade him to take an *Awake!* magazine.

'Can I have a break for a bit? I need to pop to the library,' Emily says, once the man has gone and she knows her mother will be pleased with the interaction she has just had. 'For a homework thing.' The vague lie springs easily to her lips.

'I think she's earned it, Sister,' Sylvia says to Rebecca.

Rebecca sighs. 'Be back here in half an hour.'

If she walks very fast, Emily can be in the town centre in five minutes. On the benches at the crossroads there is no sign of the girls. It was silly to follow them. She doesn't know what she was thinking. They'd never speak to her anyway. Her only friends now are other members of the community. A group of students from the local college reach the benches. One of the girls has dyed one side of her hair pink, the other blonde. She looks like a rhubarb custard sweet. She looks amazing. Emily's mother would never let her go out looking like that. She has piercings all the way down one ear. Emily is not even allowed to have her ears pierced once. Imagine having that much silver in your ear. She so desperately wants to be in their clothes, in their lives.

Two of them carry big plastic portfolios. See-through plastic that reveals tantalising glimpses of their work as they stop to chat, laugh, make plans. She sees colours and shapes and drawings of people. How do some people get to look so free and individual? Emily feels frumpy and weird in the loose-fitting, covering-up-every-bit-of-flesh kind of garments that her mother prefers.

Opposite the benches is a bookshop. Always drawn to the art, fashion and film sections, Emily makes a beeline for the back of the store. She passes a table with a display of books on offer. One is *Blonde*, by Joyce Carol Oates. Her idol is on the cover. It's a novel inspired by the actress she loves, a fictionalised take on the life of Marilyn Monroe. And it's half-price, £6.99. Emily knows that she will not be back in town until Tuesday evening, when they will go back to Kingdom Hall for more worship. At that time of day the shops are already shut. And anyway, Emily has no money. The unpaid Witness work doesn't leave any time for a paid job. Not that her parents would allow her to take on anything that brought her into unsupervised contact with the unconverted.

In that moment Emily wants the book more than anything in the world, more than the consequences for her and her family if she were to do something wrong. Like pick up the book and walk out of the shop without paying for it.

She looks around the shop. The shop assistants are all occupied: either busy with customers or talking to each other.

She decides to do what her heart tells her to do, ignoring the fear and guilt burning inside her. She wants Marilyn Monroe in her life. Before she has time to think about it anymore she takes a book from the pile, checks where people and cameras are focused, and slips it under her coat. She loiters by other tables for a few minutes to gauge if she has gotten away with her crime so far. One last scan across the shopfloor and then she walks out of the shop as casually and confidently as she can manage while she's imploding on the inside.

She hides around the corner, shuffling the book into a better position beneath her coat so that no-one will see it. Her parents must never know. She checks her watch. She has seven minutes to get back to the book stand where Sylvia and her mother are stationed. She walks very fast, as fast as she can, with one hand on the outside of her coat keeping the book safe. She is exhilarated. She feels more alive than she has done for months. She passes Kingdom Hall, knowing that when the time comes to leave home and it's finally up to her, she won't be going into that building again.

II

'What's this?'

Emily is horrified to see her copy of the Joyce Carol Oates book in her mother's hand.

'Nothing.'

'It's not nothing.'

'It's not important. Just something I was reading. For art. It was connected with an artist we studied, who did prints of Marilyn Monroe.' Emily swallows. It's only half a lie.

Her mother opens her other hand to reveal the shiny gold casing of the bright red lipstick that Emily has been trying on in secret.

Emily swallows again. She has underestimated her mother. She has been busy playing the dutiful daughter, while all the while plotting her escape from this constricting lifestyle. Emily braces herself for the fury and retribution that are sure to follow.

Strangely though, her mother doesn't seem angry.

'Look, I know you've been experimenting with make-up

and hairstyles. It's normal for a girl of your age. And I've seen your scrapbook, too.'

Drawn to the vintage glamour, Emily has been building up a style book with pictures of dresses from the 1950s, hairstyles, notes on techniques for recreating the make-up looks. Arty images. She has kept it hidden beneath her bed, never expecting her mum to go checking her room.

'But focusing on physical appearance is very shallow, Emily.'

Her mother reaches for a tissue.

It is the sadness and disappointment that are unbearable.

Then comes the lecture. 'The Bible promotes *the incorruptible adornment of the quiet and mild spirit*. Remember Peter? Chapter one. He tells us directly not to adorn ourselves outwardly by braiding our hair and by wearing gold ornaments or fine clothing.'

Emily tunes out as her mother repeats well-worn messages of submission. Girls and women are not the equal of a man; their primary role is to be a helper, not a leader or a decision-maker. A woman's ideal position is in the home. Blah, blah, blah. It sounds positively Victorian. They've been reading *Jane Eyre* at school for GCSE English. Her mother's views are centuries out of date. But Emily has no way of arguing against the Bible.

'What would your father think if he knew?'

Emily doesn't have a great relationship with her dad. She has seen him become more egocentric and domineering as time has gone on. She is now old enough to understand that there is something wrong with the way he treats her mother. Does her mother really believe all this stuff? But she's terrified of him finding out about the make-up.

'Please don't tell him,' she whispers.

During parents' evening at school, Emily sits squirming under the eye of Miss Timms while her parents patiently explain to her tutor that A-levels, and transferring to the local sixth-form college, are not really an option for Emily.

'It would simply be a waste of time.'

Given the proximity of the end of the world, according to her parents, time in college would be better spent out on the streets, converting non-believers.

The tutor is persistent. She describes Emily's artistic talent. Her studious mind. Her motivated approach to her studies.

Her mother looks thoughtful. None of it persuades her father, however. His beliefs don't support the idea of further education.

'It's playing with fire to reshape the thinking of children.'

But I'm not a child, Emily thinks. Her 17th birthday is a matter of months away.

'Besides, continual association with non-believers in an academic setting is spiritually dangerous.'

'Yes, it's a potential problem, I agree,' Miss Timms says soothingly. 'But if you think about it, it's also the perfect place for Emily to give back to Jehovah and help find more recruits. Convert them while their minds are young and malleable.'

What on Earth is her tutor talking about? This isn't the way the conversation is supposed to go.

Miss Timms explains that she herself grew up in a religious household. 'So I understand precisely the dilemma you are facing.'

Later, at school, she will tell Emily how oppressive she found her upbringing and how, as soon as she could, she left and escaped to university. Meanwhile, her tutor is artful at steering Emily's parents into allowing her to attend college so that she can bear greater witness to her faith and help convert more people.

'The A-levels are secondary, simply a means to an end for the higher purpose.' She stares hard at Emily. The penny drops that the conversation is happening on two levels. That higher purpose is not the one that her parents are thinking of.

Emily looks at her teacher with new admiration.

When she's alone with her mother, she promises that the lipstick is gone. The obsession with Marilyn Monroe is gone. She will give her parents nothing whatsoever to be concerned about. She will adhere strictly to the teachings of the faith.

'Trust me, Mum.'

While she is saying the words out loud, inside she is thinking only of freedom.

Never mind the end of the world. For Emily, this is a new beginning. September can't come soon enough.

Over the summer she strikes up a close friendship with another girl in the community, Rowena. Emily's parents approve, because they know Rowena's family from worship. Anyone from within the faith community automatically passes muster.

The friendship is good for mutual cover; Rowena sometimes pretends that she is with Emily when she is seeing her boyfriend. Rowena's father is almost as strict as Emily's, so the relationship is a secret. When they do spend time together, Emily persuades Rowena to watch all of Marilyn Monroe's screen appearances. *Some Like it Hot* emerges as her best-loved film. Even though it was made in 1959, its subject matter is suggestive enough to reinforce the myriad ways in which her parents' beliefs are so weirdly out of date nearly half a century later. They watch Liza Minnelli in *Cabaret* too. It quickly becomes established as another firm favourite.

As well as watching films, the girls also scour the charity shops, acquiring a number of items for next to nothing that Emily has upcycled on her sewing machine to convert into trendy outfits.

Rebecca seems increasingly distant and dazed, ever more under the heavy thumb of Emily's father, ever less interested in Emily herself, it seems. It doesn't take much persuasion to get her to agree to Sylvia, her mother's friend, colouring Emiy's hair. Sylvia is a retired hairdresser.

'A few shades lighter. We're only enhancing what nature's already given her,' Sylvia says, smoothing the way when she bleaches Emily's hair blonde.

With the red lipstick there is more than a passing resemblance to Norma Jean, but Emily makes sure her parents never see that. Instead, Emily looks every bit the picture of prim decorum when she leaves the house each morning.

There is a little row of garages near their house, just around the corner from the bus stop, that give good cover while she does her make-up and hair. Her signature look is the red lips, always red lips. Her hair is now shorter; she has managed to convince her parents that it would be good for college. She artfully fixes it to look more '50s with hair wax, dismantling it by the time she arrives back home.

College is everything that Emily hoped and imagined it would be. And more. It's a safe place, away from her overbearing, egocentric father. And somewhere she can reinvent herself. She meets Levi in the first week of college. They are in two classes together, Art and Graphics.

He is a handsome, dark-haired boy with hair down to his shoulders. How her parents would hate that! He has big soft brown eyes and a bohemian air. Emily likes him very much. It doesn't take long for Emily and Levi to get close.

By the end of the first term they are good friends. By the end of the second term they are an item, with Rowena now reciprocating by covering for Emily. Still performing the role of model daughter at home, Emily wears big black sunglasses, hats and flamboyant scarves when she is out and about around town. Held in high esteem by her friends for her natty dress sense, little do they know that it is mostly a disguise so that nosy Jehovah's Witnesses won't report her to her dad.

Emily continues to turn out as part of the congregation at Kingdom Hall, but always dresses down, and styles the distinctive blonde hair differently on the days she meets with fellow Jehovah's.

For a long time she manages to keep both worlds entirely separate. She knows that she won't be able to do that forever. Sooner or later someone will see her and tell her father. Or perhaps even worse, her new friends at college will see the dowdy version of Emily. But neither happens. As the months go by, the possibility of another kind of life seems more and more attainable.

Although Levi knows nothing of the kind of religious teaching that Emily has grown up with, he listens carefully and is sympathetic to the difficulties she faces in managing her dual existence. He never puts her under pressure to go anywhere or stay out late, and is never judgmental when she suddenly has to dive down a side street to avoid seeing someone she knows.

He finds a way to make it all bearable by sending her jokey notes. At Christmas, he designs a handmade card. He paints a picture of Pikachu wearing a red Santa hat at a jaunty angle, with a speech bubble: *All you missed out on was the lies about who Father Christmas was*. Inside he has written, *and the presents, the food, the tins of Quality Street, mince pies and FUN!* At the bottom he signs off, 'Love Levi'.

Though Emily hides the card, there is a terrible moment when her father finds it among her things.

'What's this?' he shouts, fingering the edges of the card as though it carries a deadly contagion. 'Explain yourself!'

Emily goes bright red. She can't explain herself. Not without getting herself and Levi into trouble. The transgression sends her father into a storm-force rage. 'I knew we made a mistake sending you to that college!'

His eyes blaze into hers. He stands in the kitchen, their dreary brown and beige kitchen with no love or joy in it, and tears the card into pieces. For a moment, Emily is terrified that he will stop her from studying at the college.

'Well? I'm waiting! Who is this boy?'

'No-one. He's just a friend.'

'Not any more. You will have nothing more to do with him. Whatever is going on will stop immediately. You will return home straight after lessons each day. There is to be no more hanging about with this— *boy*.' Spittle gathers at the corners of his downturned mouth. He manages to make the word 'boy' sound like the cruellest insult.

'Yes, father,' Emily says. Her eyes are dowcast in a gesture of submission.

'Jezebel,' he growls after her as she leaves the room.

Levi is mortified when Emily tells him what has happened. He can't believe that he is responsible for getting her into so much trouble. He understands now why it is impossible for him to meet Emily's parents, even though his own parents are willing to welcome Emily into their home.

If she continues to study, Emily's father can't stop her seeing Levi during the day at college, but it becomes harder and harder to meet socially. Their assignations are rarer and continue in secret, with ever-greater planning and ever-greater deception. Emily comes home straight away each day, as requested. She plays the role of 'good' daughter, being seen to do her homework on the kitchen table and to help with chores. On the evenings when her father is busy with church business, she offers to go and meet him, leaving early to snatch a few precious minutes with Levi first. Perhaps her mother knows; perhaps she doesn't.

The first time she arrives at the wooden gate, the huge Victorian house seems to be hiding, nestling behind shrubs and trees, their orange-red leaves just starting to drop. Once she is past them, the teal paintwork of the door and window frames against the red brick makes it look like the kind of house a child might draw if asked. She loves it immediately.

Valerie and Tim are the parents she wishes she had.

Behind the door, their home is impressive but not imposing, with tiled hallways and corridors leading to rooms that don't really seem to have a purpose but look inviting with big sofas and stunning, coordinated cushions. It manages to be both chic and homely at the same time. When Levi takes her into the kitchen Emily can't believe the size of it. She could probably fit her whole house into this space.

'Coffee?' he asks, pulling out cups from the cupboard. Emily stares at Levi's paintings. There are the recent ones from college that look like serious artworks, but there are also some that must go right back to primary school, all framed and displayed on the walls. Why couldn't her own parents celebrate her work like that?

There is a charming fireplace in the corner, with a squat log burner installed. Two well-worn but inviting armchairs sit in front of the log burner, like old friends having a conversation.

'Have a seat,' Levi says. 'Mum'll be in in a sec.'

Valerie is delightful; warm and friendly, but also bold and assertive – characteristics that her own mother doesn't possess. She instantly makes Emily feel relaxed and at home. In her own house, Emily feels on edge in case she says something wrong or lets slip some aspect of her 'outside' life.

Valerie is a lecturer in social work at the redbrick university in the city and drives a red MG Midget which, according to Levi, is a nightmare because it's continually breaking down.

'Mum has to spend a fortune on getting taxis to the train station,' Levi jokes. Valerie laughs along with him.

Her own parents would never spend money on anything as frivolous as a taxi, much less a sports car. It has been a long time since she's heard any laughter at home.

After the first visit, Emily no longer feels overwhelmed by the impressive property and becomes a regular fixture at their house. She sees less of Tim because he's a wildlife film cameraman and is often away for a few weeks at a time, shooting on location. She is impressed and excited by the freedom that his profession seems to offer. Her world has seemed so small for so long and now it is opening up. It seems impossible that there are adults this relaxed and welcoming.

'Our home is always open to you, Emily,' Valerie says kindly.

The first time Emily slips out of the house late at night to visit Levi, her heart is beating so fast she can't understand how it stays inside her body. If her father finds out, the consequences don't bear thinking about. She employs the age-old trick of leaving an Emily-shaped blanket under the bedcovers in case her parents look in. When the world doesn't end and Emily is able to slip back in unseen during the very early hours of the morning, it becomes their modus operandi. Several times a week she waits until her parents have gone to bed, then sneaks out of the house to go to Levi's.

Emily knows without question that her parents, certainly her dad, will never accept the choices she is making. She knows, too, that they would not approve of Levi, Valerie or Tim as 'people', regardless of Emily's relationship with Levi.

As the years have gone by, her father has had less and less social contact with people beyond the community, because people who are 'worldly' are categorised as bad influences or bad associations.

But none of what she and Levi are doing feels bad or wrong. Emily feels safe and welcomed – more so than in her own home. Emily starts investigating ways to leave the community. Surely, when she turns 18 in a few months' time, she can make her own decisions. Her parents will have no legal right to determine how she chooses to live.

Levi and Emily both have ambitions to go to university. Emily is clear now that she wants to go into fashion, though her parents are going to need some convincing about the value of that. If they don't support her, which she knows is inevitable, she will find a way to fund it. The college tutors are helpful and she has already begun to investigate funding and bursaries, and begins making applications for the following year. Levi has his heart set on going to Manchester to study film and television. His dad is a cameraman for wildlife films and Levi wants to follow in his footsteps. Their lives, in all their glorious creative possibility, stretch before them.

But the universe is an unkind place.

It takes a few weeks to notice, but Emily realises with horror that her period is late.

Rowena gets hold of a pregnancy test kit from the chemist, and Emily carefully follows the instructions during tutor time in the college toilets.

The blue line appears almost instantly, as she knew it

would. There is no need to wait for the full three minutes. Though she stares and stares at it, willing it to go away, it stubbornly remains. Emily's fears are confirmed. The realisation freaks her out completely. This is not the plan, not the plan at all. It's the very worst thing to happen on so many levels. For her, for her safety, for her plans to become a fashion designer, for Levi who wants to go off to uni, for all of them.

Emily and Levi skip their Graphics class and head to Wetherspoons, the only pub open at 10am so they can discuss how to handle this. They go to the bar, where Levi orders two pints of lager.

Emily offers a tight smile to the barman and says, 'Actually, an orange juice for me, please.' In spite of the rejection of her parents' faith, a termination is out of the question.

'Of course. Sorry. I didn't think.' Levi smiles his big, reassuring smile and gives her hand a squeeze while they wait for the drinks. 'It will be alright,' he says.

'Will it?' Emily says. 'You don't know my father.'

He lifts the drinks from the bar. 'Yes, it will be alright! We'll find a way through this.' The pint is bravado. Emily knows he is as frightened as she is.

They walk across the sticky carpet and sit by the window, staring out at a world that has a different filter from the one it was wearing yesterday. Whatever either of them might say, they both know it isn't going to be alright. Everything is far from alright. It's going to be hell.

Valerie and Tim are calm when Emily and Levi share the news, but not happy.

Emily and Levi are admonished about why they haven't been 'sensible about things'. They've already been over this themselves; they don't need adults berating them too. They've been as responsible about contraception as they believed they needed to be.

'Perhaps there was a split condom at some stage.' Levi thinks he can remember a time when that might have happened, but he isn't sure. It seems incredible to be having this conversation so frankly. They are words that simply couldn't be spoken in Emily's house.

'Well, what's done is done,' Tim says, with a sigh.

'Have you told your parents, Emily?' Valerie asks.

Emily shakes her head.

'Truth is always the best solution,' Tim says, pragmatically.

'Even if it's not what people want to hear?' Emily whispers miserably.

'We'll call a meeting here, and invite your parents, Emily. Seeing as we're all going to be grandparents together in seven months' time,' Valerie decides. 'We'll write to Robert and Rebecca asking them over to dinner.'

The whole thing is a nightmare, whichever way Emily looks at it. Bad enough that Emily is friends with a boy who isn't a Jehovah's Witness; that his family is middle-class with a working mother who is an educationalist makes it worse. That Emily is going to have a child out of wedlock is the end

26

of the world. She dreads the meeting, dreads her parents finding out, knows that it will be a disaster.

The reality is worse than she ever imagined.

III

The letter from Tim arrives in the post two days later, inviting Rebecca and Robert over for dinner. It sits on the doormat taunting Emily. She is on the verge of retrieving it herself and hiding it when her father bends down and picks it up, turning it over in his hands with a frown.

'What's this?'

He tears it open. Watching him, Emily feels sick. Perhaps it is the pregnancy hormones. She tries to slink away, like a guilty, scolded cat. 'I need to go to the toilet.'

'You can wait for the toilet; tell me what this is about.'

Emily looks at the floor, then all of a sudden the bile rises up inside and she vomits, there in the hallway. She tries to catch it in her hands.

'You are disgusting.'

Rebecca runs around with the kitchen roll ineffectually, trying to mop up what Emily couldn't catch.

'Have you been seeing this boy? This Levi? What is it that we have to discuss?'

Emily is suddenly mute.

A flash of realisation crosses his face. 'No! You sinning fool!'

He lashes out at her, before she has a chance to understand what is happening. The blow makes contact with her head. She falls down into the smeared sick and immediately vomits again.

Robert stands over her. 'Is this really what you've become?' He spits out angry words. 'You will not destroy me. You will never see this boy again.'

Robert's rage has further to run. He shouts at Rebecca. 'Did you know about this? Have you disobeyed me too?'

'No,' Rebecca whispers.

He swipes at her and she is not fast enough to get out of the way either. He throws the letter across the hallway.

'You sicken me. I'm going out to pray.'

When the front door closes behind him, Emily looks at her mother and sees a red mark that will no doubt evolve into a livid bruise already forming on the side of her face.

'I'm sorry, Mum,' Emily snivels.

'Go,' her mother whispers.

Emily wastes no more time. She packs a few items into her rucksack. When her father returns a couple of hours later, Emily is already gone. Tim and Valerie decide, after hearing Emily's accounts of her father's behaviour, that they will support Levi and Emily.

'I take it that means he won't be coming for dinner,' Tim says sardonically.

Emily stays with Levi and his family, knowing she is on borrowed time. She imagines her father returning home, imagines the conversations he might have had with his friends, imagines what they might have in store for her. She pictures him calling out her name from the bottom of the stairs, then marching up them two steps at a time, thumping out at the bannister like a monster after its prey. He would fling the door open, furious with her obstinacy. She can't imagine the moment that he discovers her gone, but his fury would know no limits.

He will, she knows, take it out on her mother, and Emily feels sick at that thought. But there is nothing else she could have done. Emily has to protect herself, and her unborn child, first. Her mother is a grown-up; she has made her own choice. Emily vows never to be trapped by a man in the same way. Never to be as weak as Rebecca.

Things might have been alright if Tim had not put their address in the letter. Her father would know exactly where she had gone. Where to find her.

The knock on the door occurs at exactly the time that Robert and Rebecca were invited to dinner.

What if... ? For a moment, Emily wonders if her father has had a change of heart. Perhaps they can discuss this reasonably. It's a foolish hope. The knock at the door marks the end of the relationship between Emily and her family.

Valerie answers the door to be met by what she later describes to Emily as 'five apostles'. Emily's father has brought four elders from the community along with him. Like him, they are bearded and imposing. They are gathered in the porch, and seem to move as one when Valerie opens the door.

'Yes? Can I help you?'

'Is Emily here?' Robert asks grimly.

'Yes, she is. Who are you?'

He takes a step towards her. The others shuffle forward too, their eyes gleaming with the mania of evangelism. 'Emily is my daughter and I don't have to answer to you!'

Before Valerie has a chance to do anything else, they are threatening her. First there are the accusations. Her son is a bad influence who has turned Emily into a slut. Then there is talk of Armageddon. 'You are doomed,' one shouts. Finally comes the demand. 'Emily is to come home with me now.'

But Valerie is having none of it. 'How dare you come here mob-handed, threatening me in my own home? Emily is clearly not safe with you. She'll be 18 in a few weeks and is legally entitled to decide what to do with her life herself. Please leave our property now.'

Tim appears behind her. He is less diplomatic than his wife. 'What's going on? What the fuck do you think you're doing? Fuck off or I'll call the police.'

'I want my daughter,' Robert screams.

Valerie decides the time for diplomacy is over. 'As my husband just said, fuck off.' She begins to close the door on them, forcing the men to back away.

'This isn't over; we will be back for her. We have ways of making her come back to her home where she is loved.'

'You have a funny way of showing love! Now, for the final time, leave!'

Emily, listening to every word from the kitchen, feels a chill rush up her spine. She doesn't know it at this moment, but she has already seen her mother for the last time.

IV

'Of course you must stay with us.'

Once Robert and his cronies have gone, Emily knows that there is no going back. The discussions with Levi, Tim and Valerie go on late into the night.

'We'll just have to make it work somehow. You and that baby will not be safe near those men. We'll find a way to protect you here.'

Over the next week, Tim installs a CCTV system and puts extra locks on the windows and doors. Emily is encouraged to stay inside and not to go anywhere she might encounter her father or any other members of his religious community.

'Even the voices of those men give me the chills,' Valerie shivers.

Levi and Emily are given a big room to themselves. It feels like a flat, with an ensuite bathroom and double aspect windows that have a lovely view over the fields. There is a kind of siege mentality. Levi and Tim construct a large desk for the room using an old, flat-surfaced door rested on two short filing cabinets.

Their relationship changes under the strain of the 'state of emergency' that has befallen them. Levi continues to go to college and study, encouraged by Emily.

'You can't give up on your ambition,' she insists.

But Emily herself is fearful of going outside.

It is agreed with the college, with the support of Valerie and Tim, that Emily can do most of her work from home. Valerie has an old Singer sewing machine that she inherited years ago. They bring it down from the loft for Emily to use.

There is security with Levi's family, but also tension. Emily is very conscious that, whatever Levi might say, and however positive he might be, this is not the life that he envisioned. His dream of going to Manchester to study film and TV is totally compromised, and Emily feels it is her fault. They are not love's young dream. She knows that Levi isn't ready to be a father, any more than she is ready to be a mother. How fair is it to ruin two lives? At the same time, Levi has been raised to be a good man, to do the right thing. Gradually, through morning sickness and medical appointments, their relationship changes from infatuation to one driven by duty and practicality. Levi doesn't want to touch her in the way that he once did. Emily's swelling body is an inescapable reminder of all that is trapping him in a life he never imagined.

They don't think much beyond the arrival of the baby.

Valerie, pragmatic as ever, and with a career in social work behind her, is frank with her son. Emily overhears the advice that she gives Levi.

'Yes, she's strong and amazing and a wonderful person and she's clearly done well to survive being brought up the way she obviously has, but that doesn't mean you have to marry her.'

The words cut deep, but deep down, Emily knows that Valerie is right.

V

When the baby is born, Emily chooses to name her Marilyn, after her idol. The name is perfect. Baby Marilyn has inherited Valerie's curly hair, but it isn't dark like Levi's or mousy like Emily's own original colour. It is blonde. Beautiful, pale, almost white-blonde hair. She has a little button nose and fair skin.

But Emily feels sad not to have her mother with her. She wants her mum to know. She wants Rebecca to see a picture of this perfect little girl. Levi takes several gorgeous photographs of baby Marilyn which Emily puts in an envelope with a card and posts to her parents. She still loves her parents, though she dislikes what her father has become and what her mother has become as a result. Many girls get pregnant and most stay with their families and somehow make it work. But Emily knows that can never happen for her. Still, she longs for a 'normal' family.

The reality though is that, even through the emotional turmoil of pregnancy and childbirth, she feels calmer and happier away from the family home. In spite of the overheard words, there is no pressure from Valerie and Tim to move out. They are doting grandparents, and little Marilyn is loved and safe. Valerie structures her work so that she can do more from home, which allows her to be around to help with Marilyn and relieve the young parents from their duties. Tim absolutely adores his granddaughter, whom he nicknames Mar-Mar. She lights up when she sees Grandad. He makes hilarious faces and sounds which she finds very funny. The giggles of an adorable baby make everyone laugh.

The months go by and life carries on. Levi completes college and achieves excellent exam results. The plan is that Emily will return to resit hers the following year, but there never seems enough time to pick up her studies again. From time to time, Emily takes baby Marilyn to meet her old college friends, who absolutely adore fussing over a baby. The household gathers a nice rhythm; they all bumble along with Marilyn at the centre of their collective universe. It isn't the life Emily might once have imagined, but it is a life.

The biggest sadness, aside from the dreams of working in the fashion industry being thwarted, is that Emily doesn't hear back from her parents; has no idea if they even received her photographs. It saddens Emily, who knows that her mum would have loved to hold her baby grand-daughter, but Emily knows that they have built their lives around the church and the strict rules surrounding their religion, and her transgression makes it an impossibility.

Tim announces a new documentary project that will mean him going away for three months. It's a regular aspect of his work, referred to affectionately by Valerie and Levi as 'Dad's going to sea again', even though boats are rarely involved. This time he is one of a four-person crew working in Syria, filming the animals and interviewing people who have set up a sanctuary and rescue centre there, focusing particularly on the northern bald ibis. Tim is keen to track one or two down to help promote a programme to save them from extinction.

'Isn't Syria dangerous?'

'Don't worry, I won't be anywhere near the conflict areas,' he reassures them. 'But how am I going to survive without my little Mar-Mar?' he says, tousling the baby's blonde hair affectionately when he leaves for the airport.

It's Saturday afternoon, a few weeks after Tim's departure. Levi, Emily, Valerie and Marilyn are all watching the Oxford v Cambridge boat race. Spring sunshine pours into the room. Valerie's phone rings – a number she doesn't recognise, with an overseas code.

It's Duffy, the sound man on Tim's project. Levi and Emily don't hear the words but they see Valerie's ashen face and quivering bottom lip.

Levi, sprawled on the sofa with Marilyn, stops tickling her tummy.

They all knew that there were risks attached to Tim's work in Syria, a war-torn country that has been dangerous for years. Emily knows that the call is about Levi's father. Could he have somehow been caught up in the fighting?

Valerie stares at the shaft of sunlight spilling across the wooden floor.

'Dad's dead. There was a car accident...'

She wails suddenly. A loud, wet sound that seems to release a tirade of pain. 'He goes to Syria and dies in a fucking car crash...'

VI

The wake is held at the house after the funeral. People come from far and wide to say goodbye to Tim. Being a freelance film cameraman took him to far-flung corners of the Earth and he'd been popular.

The house is already full of cards and flowers from well-wishers, but a fresh envelope lies on the mat.

'Oh, this one's for you,' Levi says with a frown, handing the envelope to Emily.

She parks the buggy in the wide hall and is distracted for a moment by the business of getting Marilyn, now quite a bonny size, out of the straps. She hands the baby to Levi and opens the envelope nonchalantly.

She gasps.

Levi, Valerie and a few family friends standing nearby immediately look over to see what is wrong. All the pictures of baby Marilyn that Levi had taken when she was born have been cut up into pieces and posted back.

'But that was months ago! Why have they done this?

Why have they done it now?' Levi is incredulous. 'And on today, of all days?'

Emily understands straight away. 'It's not her. It's my father. I think they must have made him stand down. You know, in the church. Because of my "sins". He already hated me. Now I might as well be dead.'

Silence falls on what is already a very sombre day. No-one knows what to say for a moment. Finally, Duffy puts his hand on Emily's shoulder. 'Come on, gal, don't think about him. His problem, not yours. This is where you belong.'

Emily smiles a tight smile.

'That's it, lass. Let's get back to moaning about what an old fusspot Tim was.'

Laughter fills the room and bottles begin to unclip, pop and fizz. Tim has his leaving party in spite of Emily's family's unpleasant intervention.

But life gets harder and harder after Tim's death. Perhaps he was the glue holding everything together. Valerie falls into depression, takes time off work and quickly becomes dependent on sleeping tablets and antidepressants. The fact that Tim, reluctant even to take paracetamol, would disapprove seems to exacerbate the spiral.

Levi, in the throes of grief, becomes more aloof. At the end of the first year he has the option to defer his university course, but chooses not to, deciding instead to throw himself into his studies. He spends more and more time in Manchester, away from home and from Emily and his daughter. He enjoys the student lifestyle. Emily beginds to suspect he is seeing another girl.

She, meanwhile, stops bothering with her appearance. She pours all her energy into Marilyn who, like all two-year-olds, is becoming hard work. The house is sad and miserable. Emily and Valerie become isolated from each other.

As Valerie is heading out to the shops one day, she trips over one of Marilyn's baby shoes and goes flying. An innocuous little moment, or it should have been, but it turns into the catalyst for all her grief to pour out in one huge, angry rage, directed at Emily. She asks Emily to leave.

With no family to turn to, Emily packs a bag and calls a taxi. She and Marilyn go to stay with her old college friends who live in town in a flat-share, attending the local university. At first, the girls are kind and make space for Emily and Marilyn.

But student life isn't easily compatible with motherhood. There are parties and late nights and it doesn't take long for Emily to feel she is missing out on what might have been. Gradually she begins to join in, relying on a baby monitor to be the babysitter when they go out to parties in the other flats or nip to the local pub. Emily knows it's wrong but also needs to kick up some dust and kick back. She tries cocaine, and likes it. She doesn't speak to Valerie. Things were left too awkwardly between them. When she hears about Valerie's breast cancer diagnosis she resolves to get in touch, but Valerie's decline is rapid and Emily leaves it too late.

Emily grieves her death deeply, in spite of their falling-out. It doesn't seem possible that disease has taken her. Valerie had been such an inspiration to her once, showing her what empowered womanhood looked like – when there was no role model offered by her own mother. But Valerie had given up after her husband's untimely death. How different things might have been had Tim lived.

Emily has only intermittent contact with Levi. They have very little in common these days, not even the family that once welcomed her so warmly remains to unite them. Levi, after graduation, spends some time in Salford, working in Media City learning the ropes. Although he graduated with first-class honours, opportunities in the media industry are few and far between and he can only find relatively low-paid work. He moves to London with his new partner Bethany, securing some work in advertising, mainly making budget films for car advertising. It pays the rent, but isn't the creative dream he once had. A friend is setting up a film studio in Sydney and invites him to come and be a partner in the new enterprise. Levi sees it as the opportunity to start again; to go for a clean break from the mess of his teenage life, and also to follow a creative pursuit once more in the industry he loves. He has such limited contact with Marilyn that it doesn't really make a difference if he's on the other side of the world. He sells his family home, packs up his small ground-floor flat in South London, and sets off to live in Australia with Bethany. He doesn't tell Bethany he has a daughter.

Emily is alone and desperately unhappy. It is time to take charge, to try to live the kind of life she once dreamed of. She knows that the first thing she must do is to move on from the flat share. It isn't the right environment for Marilyn.

She makes arrangements and packs up her things once more. She doesn't say goodbye to her friends, and this time she doesn't tell Levi where she is going.

With a young child in tow, Emily finds it impossible to pursue her dream of becoming a fashion designer or working in the fashion industry in some capacity. Instead, she settles for living with Jack, a window cleaner. They rent a small house outside town on the outskirts of a village. Emily takes casual jobs here and there: a few shifts in a local pub and a couple of mornings in a vintage clothing emporium. Life is disappointing. Emily is miserable. She and Jack struggle, and argue. Jack 'hasn't signed up to fucking babysit someone else's brat while she's chatting up punters behind the bar'. They both drink too much. By the time Marilyn starts school, her home life is already turbulent.

One day, when Emily is out collecting Marilyn from school, Jack phones to tell her that he's changed the locks.

'Your shit is on the drive.'

Emily is homeless once again.

There is a regular business visitor to the shop. Alan is a vintage clothing dealer who owns several shops across the region, including a stall in Portobello Market in London. He is much older than Emily, in his early fifties. But Alan has a rockabilly vibe to his dress sense, and a knowing way about him that Emily finds attractive. Moreover, he is very interested in Emily, especially when he discovers her plight.

He offers Emily somewhere to stay, in an empty flat above one of the shops. He seems totally cool with Emily having a child; doesn't run a mile as some other men have done. He turns up one night with a bottle of wine and a takeaway which Emily, stretched to the limit financially and starved of company and social interaction, finds difficult to refuse. It doesn't take long for Alan to invite Emily out, and to find a babysitter to make it possible.

'You deserve it.'

Emily decides that, in spite of his age, this is a definite improvement on Jack. After their first date, she starts paying attention to her appearance once more and deliberately ups her Marilyn Monroe appeal, since she knows that Alan is a fan.

He enjoys listening to vinyl and has an impressive music collection.

'I'd like to show it to you. Why don't you come over to mine and, instead of needing to bother with a babysitter, we can just stay at home?'

Alan lives in a large six-bedroom Victorian house in town. The interior is dark and rich. There are deep red walls, big gold-framed mirrors, and antiques everywhere. It reminds her very much of her first visit to Levi's house, one of the few places in her life where she felt safe. He makes her cocktails from the 1950s bar in the living room nearest the kitchen.

'Isn't this fun?'

Panton chairs are dotted around the two living rooms and in the impressive Shaker kitchen. Eames, Aalto, Gray, Le Corbusier, Mies van der Rohe, the artists and designers she once learnt about surround her. She feels a connection to her college days. She feels like 'herself' in this environment. After Marilyn has gone to bed, they listen to the Black Seeds and Lou Reed or other records that Alan chooses because, he says, 'You need a proper musical education!'

He has a print of Chinese Girl, a 1952 painting by Vladimir Tretchikoff that is also one of Emily's favourites. Emily falls into a pattern of staying at weekends. Alan buys her gifts of vintage dresses that he insists she wear – and also likes to see her take off.

Just a few weeks into their relationship, Alan makes a suggestion which Emily has been anticipating. 'Why don't you and Marilyn stay here properly for a while?'

She knows that this is definitely a 'strings-attached' offer, but Emily believes that she has really fallen on her feet this time. The frequent, rough sex he demands seems a small price to pay. She is thrilled that she will be living in such a remarkable house.

After a few more months he asks her to leave her job at the pub. 'You don't need the money, living here.' Emily finds this considerate, and touching. But he has another reason. He doesn't like the idea of his woman on display for other men to ogle.

She is still able to spend time working in one of his shops, but is never left alone with any young men who work in them. Alan explains, 'I want to protect my little beauty!'

What Emily hasn't expected, or understood, is that as much as Alan loves the fashion and art of the 1950s, his head and attitude to women are stuck in that decade too. Emily slips into the role of a little wifey at home, available for sex whenever Alan wants because, put very crudely, he is paying.

It is a good few years before she realises that not only does she emulate Marilyn Monroe in looks, but also in her choice of partners. She lives a life of luxury and partying and fun on the outside, that is built of inward frustration – and in frequent need of cystitis powders. Being with Alan is like being married to Joe DiMaggio. He is jealous and controlling. In totally different circumstances, she has become like her mother, exactly the thing she did not want: controlled by a man.

Her life is not her own.

PART TWO
Louise

I

Some years after

With two weeks left of the school year, I can feel the children 'letting go' already. The teachers seem determined to keep teaching until the end, but my lot already have their heads in the holidays. Sports days, concerts and activity days have disrupted the curriculum and, while school might not be quite out for summer, we're already there in the Allen household.

Summer itself, though, seems to have disappeared.

It's been a crazy year of weather, but we say that every

year. Late spring and early summer were glorious: amazing and blazing. But July has so far been cool and wet and the long-term forecast doesn't offer much promise. This will not bother us too much, though, because we won't be here. We're escaping the gloom and heading off to the sun. I can't wait. We've got a Greek villa booked, in a complex that gives us use of a shared pool, and the beach just a 10-minute walk away, according to the online details. Greece and the islands will be very hot. Some tell me too hot, but I've stopped watching the news. It's too depressing: climate crisis, war, famine, conflict. It sometimes feels too much.

Initially, it was just the evening news on television that I avoided, but now it's *all* news and news-related programmes. I used to listen to lunchtime broadcasts on the radio, but I got fed up with the way that interviews were conducted, with all the question avoidance and rehearsed shouty arrogance loved by ministers and journalists alike. So I no longer tune in. I loathe it all. Some might see this as simply burying my head in the sand. I'd counter that by saying it's part of my drive to look after my mental health. If I really need to hear about what's happening in the world, other people will tell me somehow.

The knowledge that we have just over two weeks to go until we're away in the sunshine is keeping us all going. I've been buying up sun creams, varying from SPF50 down to factor 20 in readiness. Lily and Vincent will be in factor 50 for the whole holiday, I've no doubt. The rest of us are slightly more olive-skinned. I am so excited about it. Not least because the children have their own quarters, separate from us, for the first time. What luxury. They've already had great fun selecting their sleeping arrangements from the brochure.

My friend Google tells me that there are many restaurants along the beach. I love Greek food so with the healthy diet, lots of water and swimming, I'll feel incredible and completely ready to get stuck into the new book and art projects. I've been to Skiathos before: one time with a girlfriend years ago, when we had a complete hoot, and once with Lloyd before we were married. We had such a lovely, carefree time. That's the vibe I want to capture again.

The dogs have a little holiday planned, too. They're going into a boarding place they know and love, while the cats and the house will be looked after by a neighbour, Jude. And all this rain will keep the garden going for longer while we're away. Jude will enjoy picking my dahlias from my cutting garden, I'm sure. They seem to keep flowering for months and are so much cheaper than buying flowers. A friend who did a floristry course told me to put lemonade in the water to keep the dahlias going for longer and it seems to work a treat.

So I'm feeling in a good place.

Since we went on a foster training course in 'looking after yourself', I'm a new woman. I drink much more water and am far more conscious than I've ever been of my hydration levels. I had long been guilty of the classic 'mum' thing where I would tell the children to top up their water bottles and drink two litres a day, but hadn't noticed that I wasn't doing the same. It has made such a difference to my health, along with removing all artificial sweeteners from my diet. I'd been clicking a little white tablet into my tea without a second thought. Headaches and niggles I'd been putting down to age, but this new regime is having an impact.

In truth, my exercise programme is still to be worked on. Most days I walk a mile or so with the dogs, but rainy days are a problem, and there's been so many of them. Madam Dotty, one of our pair of Jackahuahuas, simply will not go outside during inclement weather. She runs away and hides in her bed, refusing to budge because she hates getting her fur and paws wet.

I take full advantage of the final days of school to sort out the holiday clothes and begin the packing. This is less to do with being organised and much more to do with being excited. I can't wait to see the children relax and have fun in the pool and the sea. I love spending this time with them, and I'm well aware that now they're all into their teens, full family holidays are numbered. Without wishing to sound like a saccharine advert, we're making memories.

I pull all my summer outfits from the wardrobe. I think I've had some for over 20 years. The fashion companies of two of the dresses no longer even exist. Some of the styles look terrifyingly out of date, long for the sake of being long. But I have a plan. I intend to chop the maxi dresses up and make them just below the knee length. The sewing machine is already out from making Lily's new bedroom curtains. (She decided that the cream polka-dots against a pale green background were 'childish' and 'no longer relevant to my life' and instead chose plain duck egg blue fabric). I'm with her. I've become a huge fan of plain curtain material. So much easier to make: no more lining up of the patterns that, if just a little out on each side, look amateurish. Lily's curtains took less than a day to make from scratch which is so much better than the days I've spent running up complicated patterned curtains in the past. From now on, all the windows in our house will be dressed with plain curtains.

I organise my pile of dresses for cutting. A few snips and there will be no going back.

Next I take out the suitcases and bring them down to the kitchen. Mine and Lloyd's are brand-new. The children all had new ones a while ago and an upgrade for us was long overdue. My old suitcase belonged to a former boyfriend and he'd already had it for years before I acquired it. It was a very boring, sensible, grey hard plastic lump that was hard work to move. Now I am the proud owner of a stylish teal suitcase with a handle that seems to steer easily. When we park the car at the airport and do the long walk to check-in, I shall no longer struggle. The next job is to make them all easily identifiable.

I find a roll of blue and white gingham ribbon in my old craft box and cut lengths off to tie on everybody's bag to make the luggage carousel experience a bit smoother.

I'm just tying an attractive bow on to mine when the phone goes. Typically, there are only three groups of people who call the landline. Most often it's a wrong number. Sometimes it's a weird call centre trying to sell me something I haven't asked for. Occasionally it's children's social care or, more specifically, the placements team. I take a deep breath and wonder which one it will be.

'Hello, is that Louise Allen? My name is Freda. I'm calling from the placements team. We're looking for a suitable placement for a young lady. She's 12 years old. Almost 13. Her name is Marilyn. You know, like Marilyn Monroe. I've read your profile and I really think you'd be a great match for her. Can I pop over in the morning and have a chat?' She doesn't draw breath and even her question at the end sounds like a statement. I'm in a good mood and off-guard and hear myself saying 'Yes' before I've even really registered it.

'Excellent! I'll see you at 10. Bye for now!'

She hangs up abruptly, with not even time for me to finish saying goodbye. I have the distinct feeling that I've just passed through a tornado.

Lloyd walks through the back door, returning from taking out all the recycling. He sees me with the phone in my hand, no doubt looking perplexed.

'Who was that?'

'A social worker called Freda is popping in tomorrow morning to talk to us about a placement.'

We both know that 'popping in' does not have the same

meaning to a social worker as it does to everyone else. It could be hours.

'What on Earth made you say yes? We're just about to go away on holiday. The timings probably won't work out.'

'I know that. I'm not quite sure how I agreed to it. She was very pushy.'

'What do you know?'

'Nothing really. She spoke so fast. A girl called Marilyn. Funny, old-fashioned sort of a name. I think she said she was 12. Maybe 13. I haven't seen the referral yet. They're sending that through shortly.'

In the morning, the kids are packed off reluctantly to school.

'Do we *have* to go today?' Lily whines.

'There's no point. We might as well stay at home. We're not learning anything.' Vincent backs her up.

'Yes, you do. Only a few more days to go. You'll survive.'

I manage to get them out eventually. A few more days and they will require physically pushing out of the door, I suspect.

I quickly whizz around the downstairs areas with Hetty the hoover. I leave the back door wide open for some air, even though the sun isn't shining. It's one of those overcast, nothingy summer days. Days which make the thought of the sunshine and beach to come so exhilarating.

Lloyd's still grumbling about the thought of a social worker interrupting his day. 'I've got a stack of work to do and meetings scheduled all morning. I'm just trying to get everything into a position where I can get away for the holiday without worrying about work all the time. I won't be able to leave my study for long.'

'Don't worry. We'll get rid of her quickly. She's only come to tell us about Marilyn and see if we're a viable option. As you say, she might not think we are after I tell her that we're about to be away for two weeks. I'll get her in and get her settled with a coffee and then give you a shout.'

The doorbell goes, and of course Douglas and Dotty are straight on it, barking at the sound as if they are the fiercest, most terrifying guard dogs who will defend us to the death against any intruder. The reality is that they are tiny and more likely to lick a burglar to death than savage them. Still, what they lack in size they make up for in volume.

I notice that there are two people on the other side of the door, their silhouettes indistinct through the frost glass panel. I wonder if there is an assistant social worker with Freda, tagging along to learn the ropes.

On the doorstep, in front, is a woman dressed head to toe in shades of olive green. She looks smart, but it's her scarf that I notice immediately. It has accents of coral red which work well with the mossy tones. It's tied in a way that I saw years ago in a free booklet given away in the John Lewis women's accessories department: drawn up into a single side bow. It was a lovely little illustrated guide on how to tie scarves in different ways. I was captivated at the time but could never quite pull it off. It looks very smart on this woman, though, and it strikes me immediately that she is very well put together. Her hair is cropped short. It's a sensible style, but it looks great on her.

She smiles and waits for me to invite her in. She carries a beautiful tan leather handbag over her arm. It looks like a Spanish design, I notice, as she walks past me. Behind her isn't an assistant or a trainee.

It is Marilyn.

Freda introduces her breezily as they go through the hall. I close the door behind them feeling wrong-footed and more than a little put out. I wasn't expecting Marilyn, just Freda. How can we have a frank discussion about the viability of her staying here when she's present.

Lloyd appears to be slightly less busy than he suggested, and is soon also in the hall – driven, no doubt, by curiosity. He sees what I do: a young woman with shoulder-length hair, bright blonde. She is wearing a *lot* of make-up, but it is the bright red lips that stand out the most. She is sporting a short skirt and a cropped top, which together serve to show off a shapely, mature figure. I thought Freda had said she was 12. Or nearly 13. This is 13 going on 30. I'd be surprised if she is anything less than a D-cup. The whole visual construct makes me feel a little uncomfortable, as though she's just stepped from the red light district in Amsterdam into our hallway.

Marilyn and Freda make an incongruous pair. I have

to shake myself out of my sensory shock and get back to business. The dogs continue to bark and I don't blame them. They have probably never seen anything like Marilyn before.

Marilyn looks scared of the dogs, and there is a little ruthless part of me that thinks, 'Good. I can use that as a reason why we can't foster her.' My alarm bells are ringing loudly. I have two teenage sons and young Lily to think about. Marilyn looks like she will eat them all for breakfast!

Still, decorum takes over. I invite them into the kitchen. Marilyn hangs back and chooses to stand in the doorway.

'Sit down, please, Marilyn,' Freda says, cheerfully but firmly. I detect the edge of a warning sound in her tone.

Marilyn resists the invitation.

I've already felt subjected to the dominance of Freda the Fierce myself, so I must admit that I'm quite impressed by this act of independence. For Marilyn's sake it's a good thing. As a potential foster carer, however, it just ups the volume of those ringing alarm bells. This girl-woman might not be easy to live with.

Freda gestures to a seat, and I feel helpless, finding myself being invited to sit down in my own home. Marilyn continues to stand in the doorway, and I sit facing her. Freda seats herself on the other side of the table so that Marilyn is behind her. Her back is straight, her legs are positioned together and she sits perfectly upright on the kitchen chair. None of the chairs match. She has chosen to sit in Vincent's green chair, perhaps matching her sartorial colour choice. I'm intrigued by both of them. They make quite the pair. Marilyn is brave, but not so brave that she comes into the kitchen.

Lloyd places coffee cups on the table, and part of me feels relieved that it's him making the coffee. I don't know why exactly, but I have the strangest sensation that if I were doing it, it might be seen as some kind of feminine weakness. Not my own perception; I love making the coffee usually. I just sense that I would end up being judged. There is a steel frame beneath that immaculate olive outfit.

'Thank you for seeing me today,' Freda says, though the words contain not an ounce of gratitude, more a challenge.

I *want* to say, 'Yes, it was only meant to be *you*, not you and *Marilyn*, who we have no idea as yet if we could look after,' but Freda seems to be using the Force, even when she's not saying much at all, and I just nod.

'So, I'll cut straight to it. Marilyn's experiences in care thus far have been less than satisfactory. As yet, she hasn't managed to find a family that understands her.'

She allows that to hang in the air for a moment. Then she takes a sideswipe that I'm unprepared for. 'Louise, I read in your profile that you used to teach fashion.'

'Ye-es.'

'I think you two will find that you have something in common, since Marilyn is very interested in the fashion industry.'

I can tell that she has already sold that information to Marilyn, who is pretending very hard not to be listening.

'Right.'

'And of course, your record in working with young people means that you are someone who is good at understanding people.'

She manages to make what should be a compliment sound like a threat.

I look more closely at Marilyn and notice some cuts on her arms. They look superficial, nothing too serious. I know I'm projecting former foster carer experiences here unfairly. That's a fleeting observation and my conclusion is invalid. I know only too well that nothing is what you think it is, especially at first glance.

Freda is polite. She occasionally remembers that we are part of this conversation and asks various questions, but does not spend too much time listening to the answers. I also notice that Marilyn is rolling her eyes at some of what her social worker is saying. She catches me looking at her and smiles.

Now, I have to admit that is one winning smile, and I find myself responding to it, almost involuntarily. When she sees my small, disguised smile (I'm not disrespectful enough to make it obvious that I am joining in with her amusement at Freda's expense), she sees her route in. She holds up a hand behind Freda's head and makes a gesture of the hand talking. Lloyd suddenly starts smiling too; she has tapped into both of our inner 13-year-olds.

Freda, oblivious to the performance behind her, thinks we are smiling at her, and is spurred on by what she takes to be our enthusiasm. She continues to talk but with even more animation and conviction.

We're trapped.

I think I must have tuned out from Freda's conversation because suddenly she and Lloyd stand up and move across the kitchen. We're going to look at the spare room. I haven't even made a bed up. I've put all our suitcases in there with piles of clothes for each person on the bed.

'You'll have to excuse the clothes everywhere,' I say to Freda as she peers in, Marilyn standing behind her. 'We're going on holiday very shortly.'

The sentence *should* have finished, 'so therefore we can't look after Marilyn', but I'm intimidated by Freda and the words don't come out.

Instead, I hear Lloyd say, 'So perhaps Marilyn could come over when we get back?'

Marilyn looks away, out of the bedroom window at the back garden. Yesterday I mowed the lawn, which is the easiest way to make it look good. Or at least it does from the window, where you are too far away to really see the weeds. I try to look at Lloyd to make eye contact and indicate that we need to talk things over before making any rash promises, but somehow Freda gets in the way. I wasn't expecting a house tour, so I haven't closed the other bedroom doors, which normally I would have done. Details like that are my last-resort dignity hacks as a foster carer, when so much of what we do is scrutinised.

I notice that she is scanning the rooms as she walks back towards the stairs, almost as though she is making a quiet inventory. Jackson's room is diagonally opposite the spare room. Suddenly, as I look at Marilyn, I feel fearful for Jackson. With someone like Marilyn in the house he would likely grow up more quickly than I would like. In my mind, that makes the decision. She is not coming to live here. I feel more in control as we go back downstairs. Whatever Lloyd might have said, I'll email Freda this afternoon and say no.

We return to the kitchen, and this time, perhaps Marilyn feels more confident. She decides to sit down too.

'So, where are you going on holiday?' Freda asks.

Lloyd and I speak at the same time. I say, 'Greece' and he says, 'Skiathos'.

'You've never been on holiday, have you, Marilyn?' Freda says, looking at her charge. 'Imagine that.'

The way she says it makes me feel nervous.

Lloyd smiles. 'Most of the children we look after haven't been on holiday,' he says, as a way of offering consolation, rather than pity, to Marilyn.

'Your Skiathos trip sounds lovely. I went there once. Lovely little bed and breakfast place. Are you staying in a hotel?'

I answer, perfectly innocently, without thinking it through, 'It's a little villa in a group of villas.'

There's no beating about the bush. Freda says, 'Marvellous. Then why don't you take Marilyn with you?'

Before we have time to say 'beach bag', she has worked

out that we can organise a passport and that the villa accommodation is flexible. 'You can shift things about because that's all part of the fun.'

It sounds anything but fun. But it is as if Freda has cast some sort of spell. Lloyd is suddenly in the next room, on the phone to the travel agents in town to see if we can make room for one extra. Freda sits patiently while we run around arranging to take a child we don't know on holiday.

Thankfully, by the end of the conversation with the travel agent, Lloyd shakes his head. 'It looks like it would cost us another £2,000.'

Which we don't have. So this is our get-out, a perfectly reasonable one too.

'And we'd have to sleep in another villa, so that we wouldn't be with the children,' Lloyd adds, as a final nail in the coffin of what was always a ridiculous idea.

Except that, to Freda, it isn't a ridiculous idea. 'I can raise the money through business services, don't worry. Tell you what, we'll get a kitty going in the office to give Marilyn some spending money too.'

I honestly don't know what to say. All my confidence evaporates. I've been stitched up like a kipper and I have no idea how it's all happened. I smile weakly. 'Great. But could we just —' I'm about to say, 'have a day or two to think about this,' when Freda leaps in again.

'I think you can drive over to Cardiff to get Marilyn a passport.'

'I don't know about that,' Lloyd says, on the ropes as much as I am. 'I mean, we haven't got any information or paperwork. I don't think it's that easy.'

'I'll get the business team to provide you with birth certificates and all the information you need. And you can claim for the petrol, of course.'

I feel sick. Our family holiday has been hijacked. I can't believe this is actually happening. I look over at Marilyn who, to be fair to her, looks as shocked as we do.

I decide to 'do a Freda' myself: get a grip and take charge. 'Marilyn, do you *want* to go away?' I ask. Then I load it. 'With people you've only just met, to a country that you have never been to before, away from everything you know? I think that might be very difficult.'

She looks uncertain, and I think she's going to say no, but then Freda butts in again.

'Think, Marilyn, just what a wonderful life experience Lloyd and Louise are offering you!'

I might hate this woman. I certainly want to tell her to 'eff off', but I'm feeling bullied. We've been manoeuvred into such a very difficult position. Partly because we are nice, but mostly because she has said all this in front of Marilyn.

'Um,' Marilyn bites a red lip. 'I don't know. I suppose it would be nice.'

I've actually warmed to Marilyn. Her earlier eye-rolling and gesticulation now looks like a warning about how Freda is a bit much. If only I'd paid heed.

'When are you thinking of Marilyn joining us? I'd like to speak to her current foster carers.' This is an old favourite of mine. I've asked social workers before if we can talk to the previous carers, so I'm looking forward to hearing Freda's inevitable excuse for why we can't. She doesn't let me down.

'They're busy, I'm afraid. They have a big family event that they need to leave for in two days. So shall we arrange a time for tomorrow to drop Marilyn and her stuff off?'

No, we won't. If this is a game of chess, I'm ready for the end game.

'We need to speak to Moira, our supervising social worker. She likes to be here for these meetings, so I'll have to let you know if that's possible.' Check.

But I'm ambushed again.

'I've already spoken to Moira and she'll be here tomorrow for the placement meeting. One o'clock.'

Checkmate, Louise.

Now I feel like I hate Moira, too. We thought she'd left last year, but then she was persuaded to come back because they were so short-staffed. She must have been made a good offer.

'That gives you plenty of time to sort out Marilyn's room in the morning,' Freda adds, and the way she says it makes me feel as if I've somehow been remiss in using a room in my own house to start packing for a holiday.

'Right, yes, I'll –'

'So we'll get out of your way now. See you tomorrow

afternoon. I'll get on to that passport paperwork in the meantime. What a wonderful solution! Come along, Marilyn.'

It's not a 'wonderful solution' to us at all. What on Earth are we going to tell the children when they arrive home? I see Freda and Marilyn out, partly to make sure that Freda actually leaves. The only joy I can find in watching them depart is seeing the faces Marilyn makes behind Freda's back.

Bloody hell, I think. We don't even know this child. What have we done?

I wish I'd known, at that point, a little more about what we *were* letting ourselves in for.

II

By the time the children arrive home from school I'm in a weird headspace. This must be what it feels like to have been the victim of a scam, where you lose thousands and all you feel is anger and shame for being so gullible.

Fortunately for Lloyd, he's in a Zoom meeting with clients in Switzerland, which leaves me to break the news.

First back is Vincent. I think he arrives home first because he's got the longest and apparently the hollowest legs. He's straight in and straight to the kitchen. The bread bin is his first port of call. Stuffing a breakfast roll into his mouth, he heads to the fridge, breaking off a small bunch of grapes on his way past the fruit bowls. I filled all four of them up yesterday because I'm trying to get the children to eat more fruit and vegetables. Vincent and Lily are locusts when it comes to strawberries and grapes, so plenty of those, even though the price of fruit does shock me.

Next in is Jackson. He throws his bag down on the floor, one of his signature moves. His tie has disappeared and there are grass stains and mud across the back of his white shirt. He repeats Vincent's steps, though avoids the grapes.

Five minutes later, in comes Lily. 'I hate my life!'

'Lovely to see you, too,' I respond.

She does the kitchen food-hunt journey the other way, beginning at the fridge, where she takes out a yoghurt, then grabs a handful of grapes and strawberries from the bowl before moving towards the bread bin. Instead of rummaging in it, she just gets a spoon from the drawer, she chucks her bag on the floor next to her chair with all the resentment she might display if she'd just arrived to a maths class.

Now isn't the moment. I wait for the air to clear a little and snacks to be consumed. Perhaps there will be some magical transition from hungry, grumpy teenagers into personable young people who might not bite my head off when I tell them the news. Or perhaps not.

'Darlings,' I say.

They all look up.

'I have something to run by you.'

I hate this because it's a lie. I'm not running it by them; the deal has already been sealed. Right now I hate myself for being so weak and allowing Freda the Fierce to bulldoze us. Now there will be a cuckoo in our midst for our much-treasured family holiday.

Deep breath.

'Darlings. We met a lovely young woman today called Marilyn. She's ever so nice, 12 or 13 years old.' In my head

I say, 'but going on 40'. I make a mental note to find out her actual age. I pause before I say the next bit.

'And she's coming to stay for a while.'

They all look at me as if I have just said that the bananas have tickled the eggs and are about to run off with the lemon squeezer.

'Go-ood. So. She's— umm, well, she's moving in tomorrow.'

Jackson gives me a look that makes me feel ashamed. But I'm overthinking it: he just wants the crisps that Vincent has been quietly sneaking into his trouser pocket. That's what this is doing to me. It's tapped into a young, vulnerable version of me that doesn't turn up very often these days. The truth is, I'm scared of Freda. Then I remind myself that while I might have grown up in the midst of childhood trauma and abuse, and occasionally feel the insecurity that inevitably brings, Lloyd didn't. Admittedly, his parents divorced in the '70s which was rather radical at the time, but they did so amicably, and he's as scared of Freda as I am. What is it about that woman that makes us so compliant? One of her tactics was catching us off guard. I can't say that she has lied, exactly, but she certainly crafts a situation to her own advantage.

There's no sugar-coating this, so I decide to just blurt it out. 'And Marilyn is coming on holiday with us to Skiathos.'

I feel like running out of the room crying. They're going to be so angry. We've let them down because we're scared

68

and have let ourselves be outmanoeuvred by a woman in olive green with a natty way of tying her scarf. I am the worst mother and foster mother in the world. With a wrinkled brow I wait for the onslaught that is about to arrive.

Lily says, 'I'm still having the green bed though.'

Vincent, who has masterfully used my distracted state to smuggle out two packets of pickled onion Monster Munch says, 'Cool' and walks off up to his room.

Jackson, my oldest son, looks at me searchingly. I think he's going to have a go at me but instead he asks, 'Are you alright, Mum?'

'Yes,' I say. 'I'm perfecto.' What the hell did I say that for?

He walks off with the two remaining packets of Monster Munch. Why do I overthink things so much? It's because I've had it whispered in my ear by social workers for years now. *What are your wishes and dreams?* It's what they ask scared, confused, disinterested children in care in their reviews. I'm paranoid that I'm messing with the wishes and dreams of my children, but it turns out they're not that bothered. Maybe that's because they feel safe. I hope so. I look at the debris of crumbs and discarded grape stalks and strawberry tops and packets, and decide to get over myself.

Lloyd comes in after I've delivered the news. 'So, how did that go?' he asks, a little nervously.

'Weirdly easy, actually,' I admit.

He shrugs and heads to the cupboard to select some potatoes to peel ahead of dinner.

'How do you feel about all of this?' I ask him.

He smiles. 'We're screwed. That woman was a master of manipulation. All we can do now is go along with it and try to make the best of it.' His tone is cheerful and matter-of-fact.

All evening I wait for the 'but' to come from the children, but it doesn't.

And then, because they've been so uncomplaining, I experience waves of guilt. Am I exploiting their kindness, their innocence, their good-natures? Perhaps I'd have felt better myself if there had been a tantrum or two. Because so much about this feels wrong. I still can't quite believe that we've let it happen. I'm okay saying 'we' this time because Lloyd and I were definitely in this together. People's first impression of me is that I'm confident, and – dare I say it – gobby. Today I've surprised myself.

When the house is settled and my waves of guilt and fear have subsided a little, I sit in the garden with a glass of wine and ponder my feelings. They're complicated. I have a sinking feeling in my chest, compounded by rushes of shame and embarrassment. Anxiety about what to do next. Frustration about how much more the trip is going to cost us, whatever business pot they pull from and whatever 'office whip-round' takes place. Basically, I feel exposed and defenceless. Freda has tapped into my insecurities, and what's worse, she did it in my own home, my safe place.

I'm not used to being so manipulated. It's disturbing. – and definitely not the ideal way to begin a placement.

III

In the morning I feel anything but refreshed. Sleep was elusive in the night. Lloyd is up before me, already in his office working, trying to clear his in tray ready for our holiday departure.

Now that Marilyn is moving in today, I will need to move the suitcases and clothes out of her room, find somewhere else to put them, and get everything ready. That's my morning gone. And, like Lloyd, I have loads of things to sort out. I don't like the way I feel: irritable, angry, impatient, very wound-up. I add in overburdened and overwhelmed. With a side helping of anxious, nervous and a little bit afraid. I'm not normally like this. I'm good at doing life, good at staying upright. It's that bloody woman. She has set my teeth on edge. My instincts, my fabulous life-saving intuition, is screaming RUN!

All these thoughts make me more alert than I normally am at this time of day. Before I head to the coffee machine I check my emails. Moira will be here half an hour before Freda and Marilyn, who are due at 1pm. The plan is to get the formalities over before the children arrive home. That's my entire work day gone. I won't get the evening catch-up time either. I am not loving any of this. Oh, my head is beginning to ache and my neck hurts. I take a couple of paracetamol and decide that perhaps I do need some coffee after all.

I gulp it back, have a stern word with myself, and crack on. After I have shifted the suitcases and carried all the folded-up ready-to-pack piles of clothes from the bed in the spare room to the floor in our room, I hoover and clean. Then it's time to make up the bed.

Marilyn looked like she wouldn't object to a bit of pink. I have, somewhere in my fabulous airing cupboard (made fabulous mostly by the many bars of soap that are hidden away amongst the piles of bedding and throw out a stunning waft of gorgeous smells), a sugar-pink duvet set. I fling open the doors and, like a sommelier catching the nose of a vintage red, I inhale hints of sandalwood, lily of the valley, lemon and ginger, cedarwood and eucalyptus. It's a heady concoction and I love it.

There are other scents mixed in, but those are the ones I can identify. Mostly Christmas presents from Lloyd's mum, and a few friends over the years. It's not an exaggeration to say that my airing cupboard is one of my favourite places in the house. Right at the very bottom of the pile of single duvet covers I find the plain pink set, and then, from another pile, I pull out a pink single sheet to match. I'm quite proud of that pile. It's far more organised since I watched a YouTube video by an American woman explaining the technique for how to fold a fitted sheet. No more bundled up stretchy bits on display. Instead the sheets lie flat and neat. I may not be able to have control everywhere in my life, but I can at least manage it inside my linen cupboard.

I try to remember which child I originally bought the pink duvet set for. A name won't come. Perhaps because one of the first lessons I learnt after we agreed to a referral of a little girl was never to assume anything. Do not buy anything until you have met the child and learnt a little about them. You might be lucky and find that the referral tells you something nice and specific like 'they love Spider-man' or 'they're obsessed with mermaids', but otherwise you're wasting your money and may inadvertently upset the child.

I seem to remember that the little girl wanted everything to be dark purple and hated pink, so it's possible that I've never actually used this bed set before. With these mundane realisations I head back to Marilyn's room and make it look pretty. Then I have another word with myself. Pretty? Why am I saying 'pretty'? I'm making assumptions again. Marilyn as a name for a young, modern girl feels like a statement. I can see by the way Marilyn presents herself that the iconic image of Marilyn Monroe have inspired the name.

My first serious boyfriend, Tim, was obsessed with Marilyn Monroe. He had a collection of books about her and posters of her adorned his bedroom walls. His fanaticism made me realise what an enigma she was. I was never jealous that he covered his walls with images of another woman, but I was intrigued.

I remember looking at her beautiful face and, as a 15-year old girl discovering her identity (and attachment issues going on), I'd compare my arched eyebrows and widow's peak with Marilyn Monroe's. It was somehow comforting to find, however tenuous, a visual similarity with one of the world's most talked-about and beautiful women. It's a reminder of the strange space in which a child in care can end up.

Because of my relationship with Tim, I ended up watching all the Marilyn Monroe films. And I understood why he found her mesmerising. She was a woman who you could not take your eyes off. And everyone she came into contact with was touched by her. As well as being revered as a screen icon, a quick Google search will reveal the myriad of toxic things that have been said about her. After co-writing *Some Like It Hot*, Billy Wilder was asked if he would work with Monroe again. He is reported to have joked, 'I've discussed this with my doctor and my psychiatrist, and they tell me I'm too old and too rich to go through this again.'

In spite of being one of Hollywood's most powerful directors, or perhaps because of it, he is also reputed to have described her as having, 'breasts like granite; she defies gravity; and has a brain like Swiss cheese: full of holes.' Tony Curtis is supposed to have said, after shooting a love scene with Monroe, that kissing her was 'like kissing Hitler'. Elvis Presley supposedly described her as a 'nice gal' but 'a little tall for me'.

This is just the tip of the iceberg. To me, these remarks seem not just toxic, but more than a little misogynistic. I think men fear women as beautiful as Marilyn Monroe.

Joan Collins, on the other hand, revealed that Monroe had warned her about 'the Wolves of Hollywood and their depraved casting couch'. It turns out that she wasn't wrong!

My own reading about Marilyn Monroe leads me to conclude that she had a terrible life. The part that resonates the most with me is that she grew up in care. I think she's very much misunderstood. Rather than the blonde bimbo that she played so brilliantly in some of her comedy roles, she was actually a resourceful and hardworking woman. She founded her own production company that stuck two fingers up to the Hollywood studio system as it was then, and enabled her to have some control over her own career.

Beauty *and* power.

Perhaps that's what made her so threatening to men. Whatever it was, she lived a troubled existence and men were cruel to her. When I think of Marilyn Monroe I disappear down a rabbit hole of sadness. Not just for her as an individual but for girls and women in general. How, even nowadays, pretty women in particular are at first put up on a pedestal, then knocked down and treated so badly. At the same time, when I think of Marilyn Monroe I think of pretty things. Which is probably why I have been fluffing about in Marilyn's new bedroom, subconsciously endeavouring to make it pink and feminine.

The rest of the morning passes. Before Moira is due to arrive I make myself and Lloyd a sandwich. I no longer provide a free catering service for children's social care workers as I once did. If I like them, and always when children are here, I bring out the biscuits, but since the cuts to the fostering allowance, we have had to cut back ourselves.

I smile to myself, partly as a way of trying to stop myself from being angry with Moira. Where the hell was she, and what the hell did she think she was doing letting Freda come here with the full intention of moving Marilyn into our home by tricking us? I try to calm down, but I don't know if I will be able to bite my tongue when Moira gets here. I feel she has let us down. We couldn't say no to Marilyn. That would have been terrible: another rejection for an already rejected child. *Grrr.* That bloody woman, Freda!

On the dot of 12.30 there's a tap on the door. A gentle, polite sound as if the person tapping didn't want to be heard. Perhaps she hopes that we might not, in fact, hear her and she can sneak back to her car and drive away.

No chance. The dogs are straight at the front door, barking and wagging their tails. As I head for the door, I tell the dogs, 'Don't you dare wag your tails for her, she's in trouble.' As if they could understand!

I open the door wide and say, 'Hello Moira, come in.' Perhaps my tone isn't as welcoming as usual. I can tell that she's nervous, and rightly so. She should be, since she has evidently conspired with Freda to set us up. But at the same time I need to stay on the right side of Moira. She could have a negative impact on our future fostering career. If I express my true feelings about the situation no doubt she'll write it down and then it will be in black and white: *Louise and Lloyd are angry with Freda's behaviour towards them.* I know that will lead to the closing of ranks. Us against them. So, not for the first time today, I rewrite the script. I smile brightly and go through the pleasantries. 'How are you? Would you like a coffee or a tea?'

She looks at her Fitbit and says, 'Oh, a coffee, please, Louise.'

I draw on any acting skills I may or may not have and do my best. The best technique I find for hiding your anger to a social worker is to be as upbeat as possible. I also try to use the language of social care as much as possible, so that I don't, inadvertently, go 'wrong'.

'Are you excited about the placement meeting and meeting Marilyn?' is my opening gambit.

'It will be nice to meet her after reading so much about her.'

Bingo, I have flipped it. If she had read so much about Marilyn, why the hell didn't she communicate that with us? I keep calm and continue, 'In your considered professional and experienced opinion, what do you think about Marilyn coming on our family holiday?'

Take that! Straight in with the hard kick and nowhere for her to go.

Lloyd is standing in the doorway waiting for an opportune moment to tiptoe in without disturbing the flow of conversation. But Moira sees him and makes the most of the opportunity to change the subject.

'Hi Lloyd, how are you?'

Like most of the world when asked 'how are you?' he gives a naturally polite response. We all do it.

'Fine, thanks.'

I want to kick him. *Lloyd Allen, we are not fine. We're forking out money that we don't have, that will probably end up on my credit card, to take a child we only met yesterday on our family holiday. We are not bloody fine. We are furious and frustrated.*

Moira has now successfully ducked my question and fills the space by talking endlessly about how excited she is about her own holiday. She is going away this Friday for two weeks. Presumably, she is going away without the burden of an additional nearly-teenager. I think I may punch her in a minute if she doesn't stop. She goes on and on and manages to skirt around the actual issue that she should be discussing. I can only listen to it for so long before I think, damn it, I'm saying it.

'Moira, did you know that this was going to happen?'

She looks sheepish. 'Freda can be very persuasive.'

Now, isn't that just the understatement of the year? I take this as code for Moira being as frightened and intimidated by Freda as Lloyd and I were.

'So let's hear your side of things, then.'

'She told me that she was coming to see you, which I agreed to, and I said so in the email I sent to you, Louise.'

And that annoys me. Please don't begin using my name as though you are a disappointed teacher. I know when someone is trying to put me in my place. But it's not me who should be wriggling and squirming here, it's Moira. Admittedly, Moira wouldn't have known that Freda would manoeuvre us into taking Marilyn on holiday. And perhaps she didn't know that Marilyn was going to be part of that visit too.

If the idea of going on holiday hadn't been said in front of Marilyn it would have been far easier to say no. But the fact is that most foster carers are kind, generous people who do what they do because they want to see the children happy and smiling. That wonderful characteristic is ruthlessly exploited again and again by social workers and their managers.

And, of course, as she has made abundantly clear, Moira herself is going on holiday on Friday, so I guess there's not much she can or will do in the meantime.

'What about money?'

Again, she looks sheepish. 'I'm not entirely sure of the details, but I think Freda has a plan.'

I don't know if I feel better or worse. Moira is grinding my gears with her uncharacteristic wetness. Who is this alpha-Freda? How come she sails her ship so far out of legitimate waters and gets away with it? Moira is no ally here at all.

I just feel sad. Children cannot be properly safeguarded in a climate of fear. If ballsy Moira is scared, and I'm scared, what are other people feeling? This is not how we look after children. Fearful adults are not the children's friends. That cannot be an appropriate environment in which to manage children in care. We will only ever fail them if we ourselves are scared.

All too soon the doorbell goes, signalling the arrival of Freda and Marilyn. The dogs charge out to the hall, sniffing the air and wagging their tails. Part of me wishes they were a pair of vicious Rottweilers, not gentle Jackahuahuas who are smaller than the cats.

I see the blur of olive green behind the etched glass. I open the door and am immediately hit by a waft of perfume. I don't remember Freda wearing perfume last time. I'm sure I would have remembered that. Then I realise it's coming from Marilyn. Blimey, she's made an effort. She looks, well, stunning, I suppose. If she was 17. But the way she is done up is, in my humble opinion, too old for her actual age.

The rational part of me understands that Marilyn should be able to wear what the hell she wants and express herself in her own way. Her clothes are her own choice. She is her own person and she is responsible for her own body. The part of me that researches papers on child exploitation disagrees.

When I hold statistics in my head like, oh, I don't know, let's pluck one: 300,000 men are manufacturing and watching child pornography every day in the UK, then I feel uncomfortable about the way Marilyn has chosen to dress. I mean, if those are the statistics for the UK, just imagine what the numbers would be across the world. Children are being raped and manipulated for sexual abuse from birth.

I once watched a film where an 11-year-old girl was on one of those video sites that they access from their phone. I won't name it. The girl is dancing in her bedroom thinking she's dancing with her online friends when actually it is a chatroom full of men, pretending to be girls. They get her to touch herself and to parade her body. In the background you can hear her mum call her downstairs for dinner. I find our world terrifying and I don't know how best to navigate it at times. So, while I know that, in *theory* Marilyn should be able to dress how she wants, I'm also aware that her presentation is disturbing.

To me, she looks like a baby in women's clothes. Her body is closed. Her long, pale arms are folded in to her sides so that her silhouette looks like a teardrop. She is difficult to read. I'm already seeing that she is a complex individual.

I wave them in. Freda is in exactly the same clothes that she wore yesterday, which somehow makes her less intimidating. I amuse myself by thinking, 'I hope she's changed her undies.'

The dogs chase their tails around like spinning tops, waiting for Marilyn to notice them, which she does in an instant. With one hand she sweeps her long blonde hair to the side and with the other she starts petting them. She crouches down to their level. Doug is in love. He is trying to kiss her, and Marilyn giggles as his wet nose touches hers. She seems unguarded in this moment, as though there has been a tiny breach in the armour and make-up. I like this, and it gives me hope.

I introduce Freda to Moira. To my surprise, Moira stands up and shakes her hand. It's as if royalty has just entered the room. I've never seen her behave like this before. Does Freda have links to Ofsted that we don't know about? A visitation from an inspector from the Office for Standards in Education, Children's Services and Skills is perhaps a tad more likely than Freda being minor royalty. Louise, you are a cynical woman, I tell myself.

Freda wafts her hand in the direction of Moira, a bit like the Pope acknowledging the crowds in St Peter's Square. Most odd. She's a weird woman if ever I met one. Today though, I feel sound-footed and have accepted that we do not want to distress or upset Marilyn; after all, none of this is her fault and, in a funny way, I think she has the measure of Freda the Formidable, too.

Not sure what's going on with Moira. I can't work out what she's about today. Freda has clearly decided that she is the alpha-female in this tribe, but we're in my cave, so I reassert my place in the pecking order by asking Freda if she'd like a drink and then getting Lloyd to make it without even looking at him. It's quite a skill. One that takes years of marital harmony to achieve. Freda raises her eyebrows, and my nostrils widen. Meow, we're both going to start scratching each other's eyes out soon.

Then she has a go herself. She looks at Lloyd. 'Can you bring Marilyn's bags in when we've finished?'

That puts my back right up. If anybody's going to be telling Lloyd what to do, it's me.

'No, it's fine. Lloyd is very busy. I'll help you carry the bags in, Freda.'

Now that I've decided not to be intimidated, I'm quite enjoying these games. If only I'd had my wits about me enough to start playing them yesterday.

Moira, meanwhile, sits quietly, a wet rag. I notice a smile on Lloyd's face as he tends to the coffee machine. He's clocked all of this.

There is an awkward silence as we each wait for someone else to start the conversation.

After fractionally too long, Freda fills the vacuum. No further niceties today. 'You can get Marilyn's passport from Newport. I've checked.'

Yes, that's nice and easy for her to say, I think. Only the best part of three hours each way. And who knows how long waiting in a queue at Newport? Exactly what I need to be doing in the run-up to our holiday.

'Great!' It comes out so brightly that I'm sure it must sound sarcastic. 'So, what bits of paperwork will I need to get the passport?'

'The business team will arrange all the documents. You just need to collect them from my office.'

The 'just' is a nice touch. Her office is right on the other side of the county. That's at least a morning lost on top of the day I'm going to have to lose driving to Newport to get Marilyn's passport. I learn that it's going to cost £53.50 to apply for the passport.

'But it's fine because you can claim it back.'

'And will I also be able to claim the mileage to Newport and back?'

'Of course.' Freda's smile barely reaches the corners of her mouth, let alone her eyes. 'Usual rate.'

I do a quick calculation in my head. Last time I checked it was 45p per mile for petrol. Newport is about 90 miles away. Say 180 miles. That's about £80 in petrol. All I see is cost. It might well be that we can claim it back, but that will all take time. I look over at Marilyn. I wonder how much of this she is taking in. It must be so hard simply to be discussed like this, without being involved directly in the conversation. If she were a younger child I would set her up with some toys or some drawing. This is just awkward.

Moira asks about the cost of the flights and accommodation. Thank you, Moira, I think. Finally you do something supervisory-social-workery.

'Yesterday when Lloyd tried to book flights and change accommodation, the travel agent said that we are looking at around £2,000.'

'The business manager will match fund £1,000.'

Lloyd quickly jumps in. 'And where, precisely, is the other thousand coming from?'

Moira looks ashen. 'You are entitled to a holiday supplement, and perhaps you could – well, maybe crowdfund the rest or raise money some other way.'

So much for Moira's support. I think I might cheerfully murder her in a minute. I wonder what hold Freda has over Moira, beyond simply being domineering.

Lloyd is getting cross now. 'Freda, I'm sorry, but yesterday you said that you would cover it.'

She is back, quick as a flash. 'No I didn't. I'm sorry you misunderstood. I tell you what, I'm happy to personally donate £20 to help.'

Twenty pounds? She must be deliberately trying to wind me up now.

'You do realise that our summer holiday supplement is £60 per week. And it's back paid?'

Freda looks pointedly at Moira. 'Perhaps you would like to see if the Allens can claim any more money towards their holiday?'

I am, I'm going to kill her.

'Freda, I'm going to say this very clearly. We can't afford to upfront these growing costs of taking Marilyn on holiday.'

Then she hits back at us all with the big one. 'Are you saying, Louise and Lloyd, that you are going to exclude Marilyn from your holiday?'

Her pious face is looking ever more punchable, and Moira does not seem to be challenging her at all. How dare Freda? How dare Moira not intervene? I feel quite sick.

I look at Marilyn. The poor kid looks like she is trying to turn inside out. Under the mass of blonde, coiffured hair, she is quite baby-faced. None of this is her doing, I remind myself.

Moira pipes up. 'Tell you what. I'll see if we can find some emergency respite for Marilyn whilst Louise and Lloyd are away.'

Marilyn looks sad and deflated. I can't bring myself to look at Freda. This is awful.

Then Freda smiles. Her voice changes, becoming quite strangulated and weird, and more plummy. It's a voice that seems to have come from nowhere, or like she's putting it on. 'Anyway.'

That's it? 'Anyway'? Anyway, *what?* I think to myself.

She holds her hands out in front of herself and flattens down the air, as though commanding the oxygen. She's ended the conversation; she has pulled rank and patronised us all.

'Anyway,' she repeats.

I jump in. I can't not. I'm playing a wildcard. 'How would you be able to risk-assess this venture? The accommodation, for example?'

Freda takes a deep breath, as if she is bored of my annoying, pre-schooler, nonsensical 'why' questions. She looks at Moira. 'Have you got capacity?'

This is a risk assessment, not a new sofa. Moira looks at us, not Freda, while answering her question. 'Umm, no. Actually I can't do it. I don't have capacity because I'm on leave from Friday. I mean, isn't this something that business support could do?'

Oh, Moira, I think. *You very nearly did it, you nearly stood up to her.* We all know that this is the responsibility of the child's social worker. Freda completely changes the subject and says to Marilyn, 'Why don't you have a look at your room?'

Good plan, I think. Get Marilyn out of earshot while she apologises and tries to make other arrangements. Louise Allen, you are so wrong. Why do you never learn? She has sent Marilyn off to look at her room while she speed-fills out the remaining boxes on the forms. I say 'remaining' because she has already done most of it. It is like being in the estate agents or a legal office: we have little pink arrow-shaped sticky notes next to everywhere we need to sign. Moira has yellow arrows. How sweet.

'Look,' I try desperately, one final time. 'It's a big deal taking a child that we don't know abroad with us. We don't know much about her, and I see that she has been expelled from one of her schools, which suggests that her behaviour might be unpredictable or volatile –'

Freda cuts me off. 'Louise, I'm surprised. You know as well as I do the statistics about children in care and the education system. So often, they're simply misunderstood, aren't they?'

In hindsight, that's another moment when alarm bells should have begun to ring, but hindsight is a wonderful thing. In any case, Freda stands up abruptly. 'I'll unlock the car for you, Louise, so you can bring in the bags.' Lloyd's eyes are cartoon saucers, about to leap out on stalks. He rushes up to help me. We follow the Pious One out of our kitchen. I decide that I'm not letting Moira get away without joining in. I look at her and give a little nod in the direction of the hallway, saying pointedly, 'Moira, your help is most kind.'

She stands up. Like a train of serving staff at Downton Abbey, we follow Freda out to her bronze Volvo. She clicks the button and lifts the boot. We all take two bags each. There are two left. As we go into the house I see Freda standing by the boot with her hands by her side, waiting for one of us to come back and get the last two. Unbelievable! Lloyd disappears back to his study, with a polite, 'Excuse me.' Freda closes the boot and comes back inside once I've huffed and puffed my way back in with the final lot unaided.

Marilyn, freshly returned from checking out the room, stands in the hallway looking quite impish. I don't know what she's been up to, but she definitely has a mischievous streak.

Freda goes back into the kitchen, not to sit down again, thankfully, but to pick up her handbag. 'By the way, I've arranged with a charity organisation for Marilyn to start a correction programme in September. It will be every Saturday. I hear it's very good.'

I wonder if I've misheard her. 'Correction?' My face must register how flabbergasted I am.

'Yes. Marilyn will benefit from learning new behaviours. She needs to learn that presenting herself as a young lady will help her in life.'

Bearing in mind that Marilyn can hear every word, I'm just as incredulous when she continues, 'She's not particularly academic, but hopefully she will go on to do something in administration, or perhaps a vocational route. Hairdressing.'

Even wet rag Moira is speechless. This woman cannot be for real.

'Oh, and another thing,' Freda says, 'I don't know if I've mentioned it, but I only have one more week of work. My notice period ends next Friday. I'm moving to Cheshire with my sons.'

No, you hadn't bloody mentioned it, as you well know, I think. But I must also admit a kind of perverse pleasure in hearing her say this. Is Flawless Freda divorced? Unmarried? Surely not. But I don't see a ring. I know this is the 21st century but she doesn't seem the type.

'Oh that's lovely,' I say. 'How are they?'

She is quite keen to tell us that she has adopted two boys. 'I was their locum social worker and I saw their potential. Both boys are very academic and very motivated, and could become doctors or lawyers and give back to society.'

I'm standing in my hallway wondering about the ethics of a social worker selecting children in her caseload who she feels meet her criteria. The language is disturbing and smacks of eugenics.

'The youngest boy has got into a very good private school in Cheshire and the other boy is already in a different private school.'

Mischievously, I say, 'Gosh, that sounds expensive.'

'The local church is funding the costs, otherwise I wouldn't be able to afford it. Especially with the boarding fees.'

Wow. I'm shocked on so many levels and a little creeped out by the whole thing, if I'm honest. I snap out of the spell that she has cast on us.

'Right. So what day should I come next week to collect the documents for Marilyn's passport?'

'Next Monday is fine.'

Is it? Well that's all good, then. Thanks for checking that Monday is *fine* with me. This woman has an astonishing level of assuredness.

I hurry both of them out of the house before I say something inappropriate that I might later regret.

IV

I shut the door, taking a second to blow out my cheeks before I realise that Marilyn is still standing there, watching.

She is the most important person right now. I need to put the rights and wrongs of this situation out of my head. In my many years of fostering I have learnt that the children themselves are the easy bit, even when they are doing the most outrageous things. I can accept that behaviour because I *get* them. I understand trauma.

The hard bit is working with the professionals and bolt-on services. It's the adults, not the children, who are the problem. One job I never want to do is HR. I was a union rep for a while and that made me realise just how difficult people can be. So, hard though it is, I push Freda and Moira from my mind and concentrate on this young person.

Marilyn has a beautiful face. I would love to see her without the makeup, but it's her choice, her 'hoodie' to hide beneath. Today she does look a little like an American beauty pageant contestant. She has a quite incredible figure for a young teenage girl. She must be 13, surely. An 'early developer' would be a good way of describing her. Unlike Lily, who is a similar age but still hasn't qualified for a bra yet. We have bought some starter bras with a little padding that make her feel more confident. I wonder how Lily will get on with Marilyn.

I smile warmly at the new arrival. 'So. Are you hungry?'

'No,' she shakes her head. I'm not surprised. It's rare for a child to eat after they've just arrived. Their poor feelings are spinning all over the place.

'In which case why don't we go and sort out your room, and then we can have a proper tour around the house.'

She nods. 'Thank you.'

For a girl who, according to her referral, can be 'adventurous' she is behaving very meekly. I have to say that the word 'adventurous' did leap out from the page and grab my attention. I wonder if perhaps that was the most diplomatic way of saying 'wild'. We learnt a long time ago to be wary of the term 'lively' for obvious reasons. 'Lively' sounds like a nice descriptor, but what we often end up with is the extreme end of 'lively'.

We gather up her bags, and one large, very old and shabby-looking suitcase held together with brown parcel tape.

'Lloyd, can you give us a hand?' I call.

He happens to have just finished a work call. 'I timed that wrong, didn't I?' he jokes, picking up the big suitcase and teasing Marilyn in that 'dad' way. 'Blimey, Marilyn, did you pack a load of rocks in here?'

She smiles and plays along, humouring him, which is sweet of her. The other children tend to just roll their eyes and ignore him, except for Vincent who I think has caught on to the silliness of Lloyd's jokes and rather likes them.

As we enter her room I ask if she is happy with the layout. 'It's quite easy to shift things around.'

She squints, assessing the room. 'Do you mind if we move the bed to behind the door?'

I understand that. She is not a young child and no doubt feels the need for privacy. Lloyd and I move the bed across the room. I pull the gold Ikea rug to cover the new space and shuffle the painted Loom chair about. 'Hey presto, will that do you?'

Marilyn is pleased. 'Perfect!'

Lloyd goes back downstairs to his office once more.

'Is it okay if I help you unpack?' I ask, carefully.

She looks a little confused. 'Yeah, sure. If you like,' she shrugs.

I open the big old suitcase and pull out an array of vintage and modern dresses. She's not short of clothes, that's for sure. I often find myself purchasing clothes for ill-equipped new arrivals. There will be no need for that this time. In fact, I'm not sure if the wardrobe will be big enough.

I find myself sitting in the chair, passing up the dresses to Marilyn, who hangs each one on a coat hanger, straightens it out lovingly and then lifts it up carefully on to the wardrobe pole, arranging them by colour. I share her love of clothes and have my own collection of vintage items.

'I've got a Mary Quant dress that I found in a charity shop in Oxford,' I tell her, 'along with a couple of Ossie Clark pieces. I'll get them out later and show you.'

She nods enthusiastically.

This feels like a really good start: day one and within the first hour of her arrival I'm bonding with Marilyn. Okay, I admit to myself, what is actually happening here is that I have, for the first time in years, got a female in my life who gets as excited about hair, clothes and make-up as me. Marilyn, despite being so young, not only knows about but also appreciates Coco Chanel, Christian Dior, Pierre Cardin and Yves Saint Laurent.

'Do you think Freda was inspired by Yves Saint Laurent?' I say, with a hint of mischief.

She smiles. 'In what way?'

'He wore the same suit every day.'

She laughs, instantly getting what I mean.

'He had a room full of identical clothes, and chose a fresh one every day.'

Marilyn giggles. 'I don't know if Freda wears a *fresh* suit everyday,' and waves the air in front of her nose.

I smile, but change the subject before I am encouraged to enter into a bitch fest. It wouldn't take all that much. I'm still feeling the spikes from Formidable Freda. For some reason, the words echo in French in my head. *Freda Formidable*. Could be a French fashion label.

Once we have finished hanging all of Marilyn's dresses, which takes a good while, and I have ordered a clothes rail online to accommodate the next bags of clothes, we go through them anyway and decide if anything needs washing, airing, ironing or throwing out. There is no more room in the wardrobe to hang anything else. But I acknowledge again that I'm rather enjoying myself.

Marilyn has a way about her that is captivating. Her voice is husky and seductive. It's a voice that will serve her well later in life. She would sound good on the radio. But she looks good too. She is naturally graceful and holds herself well.

As she pushes the old suitcase out of the bedroom door, I think again how tatty it is. She'll need a better one to take on holiday. I go downstairs and return with laptop. We look at suitcases, the same ones as the others have.

'Are you sure?' she asks, before choosing the red one. I'm a little annoyed with myself that I presumed she would choose pink. But actually, if I look at her clothes, there is no pink. It's weird, because if you picture a girl like Marilyn in your mind, pink is the colour that pops up. That means that I'm hardwired into the marketing of girls' rubbish, I scold myself.

She tips her jackets and coats out on to the floor; she certainly has a diverse collection here. I go back on my laptop and order wardrobe and rail fresheners. There is a trace of 'vintage' odour, which is fine and reassuringly familiar, but I think in this room with the door closed, it might potentially be overpowering.

Marilyn holds up a jacket. It's a style that I remember being popular in the '80s: stone-washed denim.

'I have a pair of jeans that go with it,' she says, when she sees me looking.

I think of Shakin' Stevens wearing his trademark double denim. I ask Marilyn her thoughts on that particular look.

She chuckles. 'Mum said a very firm "no" to double denim, but I like it. I have a red bag that goes brilliantly with it.'

In the referral it says that Marilyn's mum 'couldn't manage' her daughter's behaviour. Marilyn has brought up the subject of her mother, but I don't want to push my luck as we sit here marvelling at clothes by ruining it with conversations that will no doubt be painful. That can wait. But as Marilyn mentioned her mother, it feels okay to mention her too.

'You probably get your fashion sense from her, I imagine. As well as your good looks.'

Marilyn smiles and looks back at her jeans. Perhaps she is a little rueful.

No matter what has happened in the past, no matter what a child may say in a heightened state of emotion, and no matter what is said by social workers in reports, I have never met a child without an emotional attachment to their mum. Sometimes in the most diabolical of situations, no matter how inappropriate it might seem to an outsider, it is natural for a child to want their mother. I've learnt to keep a very open mind about this.

As a foster carer, I can't take the place of a mother. I'm here to do the best I can, to do right by the child. We never know how long a child will be with us, or how quickly they might leave. Pretty much all the children I have looked after make their way back to their birth family at some stage and, since the ubiquity of mobile phones, it's important never to think that the family is not 'with' them in some form – and therefore with me also, to a certain extent – while the child is in placement.

It's my job to help keep the airwaves open and, as much as I disapprove of, dislike or fear a parent, I can never pass judgement. I have to be bland, the grey rock. When we began fostering,I was cross with mums who hurt their children – perhaps because of my own childhood experiences. But now that I'm longer in the tooth I know only too well that people aren't always who they say they are and things aren't always as they seem. I now take the view that we need a pair of tweezers and a decent amount of time to try to unpick what has happened to these children, what it is that's gone on in the past and is informing the present. And the reality is that we will only ever know a little bit of it, and have to be content with that.

The afternoon soon runs away in a swirl of fabric. We

have emptied out everything apart from one bag, a black Nike sports holdall.

'Last one and then we're done,' I say to Marilyn.

Her face changes a little and those beautiful blue eyes flash a look. I can't say exactly what it is, but I know that something isn't right. She is uncomfortable.

'But how about we take a break for now and have a drink and something to eat? The others will be home before we know it.'

She smiles. Relief.

As we head back downstairs, I realise that I haven't given Marilyn the tour.

'I'll just show you where the downstairs loo is, if you like.'

She smiles and nods. I walk her up the corridor towards the toilet. It's opposite my studio and has a large sink, so doubles up as a paintbrush room. She goes in and closes the door behind her. I make it obvious that I am not outside. 'I'll just be in my studio, Marilyn.' I hear a little 'thank you' from the other side of the door.

My phone is still on charge and I haven't looked at it for hours, not since before Freda and Moira were here. I pick it up and see many messages. The one that catches my attention is from Moira.

Hi, I hope everything is going well with Marilyn, please call if you need anything, I'm away for two weeks, this is the number for out of hours and emergencies, I'll call you tomorrow.

Untypically thoughtful. Looks and sounds like guilt to me. I like Moira and have worked well with her in the past, before she left the first time. Things have been more strained since she returned. I try to give her the benefit of the doubt. It must be weird coming back again after you have done your goodbyes. I've noticed a few social workers have come out of retirement to return to the frontline recently. I suspect that they are very good, actually. I think, knowing what I know, you need people who are tough and resilient as well as being kind at the coalface.

From my perspective, it seems that newly qualified social workers do a couple of years then move on to management roles. Perhaps they struggle with the sheer magnitude of what child protection means in practice. But the younger managers, with only a few years in the field, lack hands-on experience, which explains why some of their decisions and ideas seem a bit strange. It should be the other way around: experienced well-paid staff on the frontline making the big decisions and the cheaper, less experienced staff doing their administration. I take my hat off to these social workers, even if I sometimes lose patience with them. It's a tough, tough job.

First child back home is Lily. No after-school hanging around and chatting for her today. Instead she has rushed home to meet Marilyn. Though of course she is way too cool to actually admit that. She comes through the door to see us standing in the hall holding a few items of clothing that Marilyn wants to wash.

'Hello, Lily, meet Marilyn. Marilyn, meet Lily.'

Two awkward 'hellos' echo around the hallway. Even someone like Lily, who came here herself as a foster child years ago and must remember what it's like, finds this part awkward.

'Lils, why don't you grab a drink and a nibble and show Marilyn around the house?' I know that she loves doing this. She could work for any estate agent and do them proud. It's a good thing that I didn't manage to take Marilyn on the tour. This is a nice way for them to break the ice. The girls walk ahead of me. I follow them into the kitchen where we are suddenly met with a loud yap from Dotty. Before I have time to say anything, Lily is explaining.

'Don't mind them. It's Dotty and Douglas's dinner time and Dotty is very bossy.'

Marilyn giggles. 'Just like Freda, then.'

I nearly smile, but resist and just say, 'Yes.'

The multipack of purple Monster Munch was replenished by Lloyd earlier today, so there are ripe pickings. They take a packet each and sit down after Lily makes them drinks, adding copious amounts of ice to the glasses.

I do my usual 'I'm not here' thing, doing my best to fade imperceptibly into the background. I think I just sort of disappear in the minds of the children. They forget that I'm listening as I unload the dishwasher, wipe the surfaces, spray anti-bac (because I know that those pesky cats will have walked across all the surfaces, even the hob to search for cheese crumbs).

I hear the door again and two laughing, loud young men come flying into the kitchen. They see Marilyn and suddenly go quiet. Oh my, she certainly has a power. In the vicinity of the wrong boys or men those looks could be exploited. Jackson and Vincent edge their way around the kitchen with a delicacy very different to yesterday when our guest wasn't present.

They find the Monster Munch and get drinks. Vincent will only drink water. He has decided that this will be the magic bullet that will prevent him from getting spots. He found something on his phone that explained the power of water. I'm fully supportive of this and must say that his skin is looking most plump and peachy. I have no idea what Marilyn's skin looks like under her beautifully-applied make-up.

'Jackson, Vincent, this is Marilyn.'

They both say 'hello' in new, deeper voices. Interesting. They leg it out of the kitchen as soon as they can.

I call Freda's office and arrange a time to meet her there on Monday in order to collect the documents to take to the Newport passport office, as she has decreed. I can't speak to Freda herself, but I leave a message explaining that I'll have Marilyn with me since we've all decided that there is absolutely no point in sending her to school for the last few days of term.

I leave Lily and Marilyn to it in the kitchen as I shoot around the house making it evening-proof. I would love to sit outside but it's just not warm enough and the sky is grey. I make sure that the upstairs bathrooms are clean and tidy and that the boys are okay. They are in their separate rooms gaming with each other, eating crisps and anything else they smuggled out of the kitchen.

I walk into Marilyn's room with a fresh towel that I promised her. I've chosen a red one. I straighten the chair and notice that the Nike sports bag has been moved. I look under the bed and there it is. I won't be nosy, that would be very rude. She probably has her personal stuff, maybe things from her mum and family. Or sanitary towels, that sort of thing. I must remember to check with her if she needs anything like that. It's hard coming into a new home and having to ask for basic things. I never like to presume, but with girls I always leave a few towels in a bag in the sock drawer.

As I return downstairs, I can hear Lily talking 10 to the dozen at Marilyn. She is so excited to have what she always hopes will be a new friend. Friendships are so precious.

Not so long ago, Vincent turned my world upside down. He didn't mean to and was only giving an honest answer to my question. I asked him why he didn't hang out with a friend of his that he'd been very close to at primary school. His friend would come over for sleepovers, though never the other way around. His friend was here quite a lot actually. We knew that there were problems at home and I think he enjoyed the security of being here. Vincent stayed friends with him until Year Seven, then suddenly he stopped inviting him over. I felt sad for this boy. I knew he loved coming over, and I fed him well. I knew he was hungry and neglected. But Vincent said something that shook me.

'I don't want to be friends with people who have issues themselves. You know, because we foster and we're dealing with that all the time. I want a break.' He sounded weary. Old beyond his years. It's probably a very perceptive thing to say, but it genuinely rocked me, and it's another one of the many reasons I'm so agitated by Freda, and by Moira's lack of support. Moira knew that about Vincent, because I told her. I'm constantly worrying about how fostering will impact the boys. It's a tough line to walk.

I have a feeling that this particular foster placement may well have a significant impact – on the boys in particular.

V

The first week with Marilyn goes reasonably well.

Then, at the weekend, Lily, Marilyn and I take a trip to the beach. Just the girls. Marilyn looks very stylish. She sports big black Jackie-O sunglasses and has worked hard on her hair. The style today is slightly bouffant. She has certainly learnt the art of backcombing those blonde locks for added volume. She wears ripped denim shorts and a white crop top. The jean shorts are cut high to show off bum cheeks. Lily initially comes down dressed in leggings but, after seeing Marilyn's attire, she dashes back upstairs to put on a pair of shorts. Hers are khaki and a more sensible length. Of course I don't say anything, but next to Marilyn they seem a bit Scout-leaderish.

As we walk along the promenade enjoying the (rare) sunshine, Marilyn turns heads. There is no doubt about it, she has 'it', whatever that may be.

It's quite a phenomenon. And I think I find it a little bit terrifying in someone so young.

I catch Lily noticing how Marilyn walks and trying

to emulate it. She slows her pace and develops a bit of a swagger, and I suspect she is enjoying the secondary attention she receives from being in Marilyn's orbit. I walk alongside the pair of them like a bodyguard, ready to leap at anyone who says anything. I can't start ribbing people about how they look or I would sound like a mean girl in the school corridor, but just let them dare to say anything. We stop for an ice cream and then carry on along the prom until I decide that enough is enough of men looking at Marilyn. Licking the ice cream seems to be seductive, so we sit down on the beach and I put up the windbreak to avoid the ogling. For God's sake, what is wrong with them?

Marilyn can't be oblivious to the effect she has on people, but she seems indifferent to it at the same time. It's certainly a complex world to navigate. Women are conditioned to cultivate male attention. I can see how perhaps other foster carers may have found being around Marilyn 'challenging', but it's more complicated than teenage defiance. The way she looks, which she certainly cultivates, must contribute. As for Freda the Fierce's correction programme, stuff that. I'll do everything I can to make sure that doesn't happen. Why don't men correct themselves, eh? Remove the girl or woman because men can't trust themselves. Is that really the answer? I like Marilyn. I like her swagger. I admire her. As we sit on the beach and talk, I ask her about her name.

'Where does it come from? Were you named after Marilyn Monroe?'

She sighs. 'My mum is the world's biggest fan of Marilyn Monroe.'

I quietly disagree. She hasn't met my old boyfriend, Tim. Not to mention the millions of other people who have been captivated by her.

I encourage her to talk further. I know that Lily has already been researching Marilyn Monroe on her phone last night. Marilyn tells me that her mum, Emily, wanted to study fashion at university. 'But getting pregnant with me stopped her from doing that.'

I'm full of sentimentality from when I ran the fashion course at the university myself. I remember, with a good deal of affection, my own students. Some did occasionally drop out because they became pregnant. So what? I have no doubt they carved out good lives for themselves. They were remarkable young women. As, I suspect, is Marilyn. She's certainly very switched-on and articulate. I am growing very fond of her very quickly. I sense that she has hidden depths. Perhaps I'm biased because she loves clothes and knows so much about them. She does have a mobile phone that her mum gave her, which I hope won't become an issue. Of course, having a phone has become standard, especially for a child of Marilyn's age. The ubiquity of mobile phones among the very young is one reason why fostering has become even more challenging. Sometimes the parents listen into conversations and sometimes, if children are being mischievous, they will set you up to say things that their parents may record and report. I've learnt that the hard way.

Marilyn certainly has power, a huge amount of it. Ice creams finished, we carry on our walk. She almost struts along the promenade. I walk behind, watching how people react to her. It's funny how both men and women struggle with confident women, even if they are only teenagers. I don't think I want to encourage Marilyn to walk around town in those shorts, though. It's okay here: we're by the sea and I'm around to protect her, but shamefully, we still live in a world where women and girls are routinely objectified and sexualised.

If you watch young girls together, they love dancing and singing and dressing up – but through the lens of the wrong people, their natural, playful behaviour becomes the voyeur's sexual interest. As my adoptive mother Barbara would say, and quite loudly while out in public, 'Bloody men!'

But when Marilyn arrived that first day with Freda, I saw a vulnerability in her. Unsurprising, given that she was in a new house with complete strangers and Ms Bossy Knickers, God's gift to social work. So, like every woman I have met, I know there is always more than meets the eye. Marilyn is not a straightforward individual. A tough exterior, resilient demeanour, and confident strut no doubt act as a carapace for whatever is going on beneath.

Marilyn seems to enjoy our beach day, and we have a lovely weekend overall. The boys actually manage to speak to Marilyn, who introduces them to gangsta rap and Katy Perry. They are smitten, as everybody seems to be who comes into contact with her. I think, in a funny way, she might already be helping Jackson, naturally shy, to have a little more confidence. She is definitely responsible for giving him a bit more street cred.

They go to the shops together and Jackson reports that his friends have been messaging him, desperate to know who the 'hot girl' is. He very sweetly replies, *my new sister*. I smile at that. Not 'foster' sister. There is a nice atmosphere in the house, and they seem to all enjoy hanging out together, becoming good friends. Lily has taken to wearing red lipstick, which I'm not too sure about, mainly because it's the wrong shade of red for her complexion. She needs an orangey red – unlike Marilyn who can carry off the classic ruby with aplomb.

If this lasts, then perhaps I can have high hopes for the holiday. I push the worrying costs to the back of my mind.

VI

On Monday there is more enthusiasm for school than there was last week. The children are ready in good time and no-one is complaining. The countdown to the holiday has begun in earnest, and there is genuine excitement about going to Skiathos. I am instrumental in whipping up the excitement, and probably the worst of the lot of us.

We never went on holiday as children, aside from one regular trip from Oxford to Fishbourne near Chichester to stay with an old neighbour and her family. I think perhaps she was the only friend Barbara, my adoptive mother, had in the village. They gave me the heebie-jeebies; the mother once forced my hand on to her big Bible in their dining room that looked like a church. She wanted me to confess to a crime I did not commit: the theft of a packet of marshmallows from the kitchen cupboard. I would not put my hand on that Bible. I was eight years old and not impressed. Now as an adult I make up for the lack of vacation excitement as a child and work myself up into a frenzy.

But I must put all that aside since today is the day that we head cross-county to the office of the lovely Freda to get the paperwork for Marilyn's passport. Calling her 'lovely', even ironically, doesn't eliminate the slight trepidation I feel at the thought of being in her company again. On the upside, the car journey offers a good opportunity to chat. All the best conversations happen in the car. I think that's what they were designed for. Otherwise there would only be one seat in the front. That's my view.

Time is running away with me now. I plan to try ensure that the lion's share of my work is done on Wednesday, after I've got Marilyn's passport photos done and driven to Newport to collect her passport. Once I have the paperwork this morning we can call into the supermarket where they have a photo booth and I can get Marilyn to pose for her photos. That'll probably be another £6 or so. I'll explain in the car that she needs to have her hair off her face and no pouting or big jewellery. She needs to practise making a poker face. I've heard Lady Gaga playing as I go past Marilyn's room, so I'm hoping it will be a familiar concept.

It's warm but muggy today. I fill up a couple of bottles with water and, once the house is clear of post-school-departure chaos, Marilyn and I start our journey to see Freda in her office. The miles pass quickly. Marilyn is lovely company. We talk about all sorts of things. She's very mature and very bright and at times it is simply like talking to another adult. Without much prompting, she begins to talk about her mum.

What becomes clear very quickly is how much she loves her mum. It breaks my heart how children end up being separated from parents who are good people at heart. Life is mucky and murky and sometimes it can be too challenging for families. I had already learned that Emily had Marilyn when she was a college student. Now I glean that after things didn't work out with the father, her mum had a few boyfriends but nothing really serious until she met Alan when Marilyn was still quite young.

'How do you get on with Alan?' I ask.

She shrugs. 'He's okay, I suppose. But I don't like the way he controls mum.'

My ears start flapping at this. The cartoon version of me would look like Dumbo. 'Oh really? That doesn't sound good. How does he do that? How does he control your mum?'

Marilyn laughs. A hollow laugh that shouldn't come from a 13-year-old child. 'Money. What else? Same old shit.'

I have to remind myself that I am listening to a young girl. She sounds like an embittered, middle-aged woman who's learnt about life the hard way.

The old side-by-side in the car trick works and she opens up further. 'He's rich. Or he says he is. Houses and shops and stuff. He's a bit of a dickhead.'

I do some sensible, middle-class tutting. 'I'm sorry to hear this, Marilyn. How do you feel about how he treats your mum?'

She starts picking invisible specks of something at the corner of her phone screen protector. 'She likes him, so I guess I have to be happy about that. But she's not my mum anymore.'

I've heard children say this before about their parents when they are in relationships. I know that people can change when they meet someone new and become involved in a serious relationship but, in my experience, when they change dramatically, that's usually a warning sign that something is not right in the dynamic of the relationship. Perhaps there are elements of coercive control. In the last decade or so, since the concept of gaslighting entered popular consciousness, I think many more women are aware of the dangers. Not just the victims themselves, but those who care about them, too.

I wonder what else has gone on for her. I sense that I'm not getting the whole story here. She flicks on her phone and puts on Zara Larsson's *Lush Life*. Marilyn looks a bit like her, actually, but if pushed, I'd probably say Marilyn is even more stunning. She car-seat dances with her arms in the air, and is mesmerising to watch. I struggle to keep my eyes on the road. She definitely has a way about her that seems a bit magical; the sort of grace and movement that many would have to practise and take a long time to learn – but not Marilyn. She embodies what it must mean to be 'born with it'.

I want to ask about Marilyn's dad, but we run out of time. According to the satnav we 'have reached our destination.' I drive around the block a few times, unsure where the offices are actually located.

'I don't suppose you know?' I ask Marilyn. Of course she does. She is a seasoned visitor to this place and easily points the way. The offices are in the industrial estate next to the road. I didn't expect that. We drive past a burger van on the corner, and a tyre repair centre, around the corner and here we are, outside the most unexpected industrial unit, Children's Social Care on a discreet sign. Not much parking so I bump the car up on to a grass verge, and think 'whatever'.

In the reception area are a number of adults who look like they could be parents waiting to see social workers. If that sounds like a sweeping generalisation, it is. I see a few children; one I recognise. He was placed with a friend of mine, Shelly, a while back, but he was off the scale in terms of behaviour. She is an experienced foster carer and yet could not manage him. I was round at their house during the AGA oven-destroying incident, but that's a whole other story. He doesn't recognise me. I remember discussing his situation at length with Shelly at the time. We both knew he needed something much more than a regular foster placement but instead he was being bumped around the system to different placements where people couldn't manage him. All that achieved was hardening his anger and pain. And now here he is... again.

Seeing him here brings home to me what a weird sector

– or industry, since we are on an industrial estate – this is. Effectively, he is in the 'returns' section, while I am in customer services.

In the queue, Marilyn and I are the same height. She looks like she will get taller, too. We stand a good distance from the people talking to the receptionist as a matter of courtesy. I want to give them space and I don't want them to think I'm listening; although, to be honest, you could hear them down the other end of the street. When they eventually sit down I approach the lady behind the counter. She has very long, dark hair, so long that she could sit on it. She looks like Rapunzel without the 'gold'.

'Hello, we've come to see –'

Before I finish my sentence, she looks up at Marilyn and cuts me off.

'Freda?'

I didn't realise Marilyn was so well-known, but she is quite unforgettable.

Dark Rapunzel looks at her computer screen, then picks up her phone. 'Marilyn and her foster carer are here to see you.'

We take the cue to sit down but there are no seats available, so we hover by the entrance door. Marilyn holds up her phone and flicks through it. She must have lots of friends: it's always pinging. That's girls, though.

I spot the olive-green vision as she heads along the corridor towards us. She whisks us off efficiently to a side room. While we sit down, she puts a brown A4 envelope on the table and pats it with both hands. She smiles, looking very pleased with herself.

'Are you excited, Marilyn?'

'Yes, very much. Although there was a plane crash last week. Did you hear about it? Just came down in the ocean a few minutes after take-off. No survivors.'

She hasn't mentioned any concerns about flying to me, but this isn't good to be focusing on.

Freda loftily informs Marilyn that she is more likely to get run over by a car than killed in an aeroplane crash.

I sit quietly, wishing that they would end the conversation, wondering whether to intervene. What would Freda do? She would take charge.

I can't resist a sweeping, drawn-out, overly-dramatic 'Anyway,' with a slightly teacher-esque tone to end it. 'I'm sure Freda has plenty of other things to think about and a lot to do before she leaves.' In my head, I add, 'like ruin more family holidays and put people into debt', but I keep smiling cheerfully. As if she can read my mind, Freda pulls a £20 note from the pocket of her olive jacket with a theatrical flourish.

'As promised. I am a woman of my word.'

Aren't you just? And one that obviously does not understand the cost of a holiday. Nevertheless, I pocket the cash.

Once Freda has finished lecturing Marilyn on air travel

and life in general, she pushes the envelope over to me with the tips of her fingers, as if it is my next secret mission. The theme tune to *Mission Impossible* runs through my head. And intensifies when she doesn't quite take her hand off it as she speaks.

'Everything you need to know is in there. You can gather the passport requirements from the information it contains. Did you bring two passport photos?'

'Sorry, what?'

Freda looks indignant. 'We need two passport photographs to be kept on file. The business manager will need to write you a supporting letter to take to the airport. They won't let you through customs without it, which is why we need the photos.'

It would have been nice to have known that before we bloody well came here. 'I'm sorry,' I find myself saying, even though it's the first I've heard of it and I have nothing to apologise for.

'You're creating a great deal of extra work, you know.'

So are you, I think. You're the one who's put me in this position.

'Don't worry, you can drop them off tomorrow.'

Can I, indeed? Well, thanks so much for that. That's another two hours' extra travel on top of my six hours to Newport and back. But don't worry, I've nothing better to do in the run-up to my holiday. Of course, none of this internal monologue is shared.

Freda stands, signalling that the interview is over. I rise too, with the envelope in my hand.

'By the way,' Freda announces. 'Today is actually my last day, not Friday.'

I don't think I could dislike her anymore if I tried.

'I see. In that case, can I have a name, email and number for your head of business services?' A not unreasonable request, surely.

Freda frowns. 'You can get that at the front desk.'

She walks up to Marilyn and hugs her, then strokes her hair like she's a baby. Marilyn stands still and chews her fingernails. Then Freda turns on her heel and disappears. I am reeling, but my emotions quickly solidify into anger when I see that the queue in reception is now almost out the door.

We join the queue once more and wait for about 15 minutes in line to speak to the lady with the long dark hair. I'd like to say that we wait patiently, but I'm short on that particular quality this morning.

VII

When I get home I am still smarting from what feels like needlessly callous treatment. I don't want to voice my opinion in front of Marilyn because that would be inappropriate, but, once she goes upstairs, I find Lloyd in the garden loading up the compost heap and he gets both barrels.

My retelling comes out in thick, fluent 'dockyard'. I mind my language in front of the children, but now and again, in certain situations, I find that a choice swear word is the only thing that will do. I'm sharing my feelings. Isn't that what we're told to do?

Lloyd looks confused. 'What's in the envelope?'

I haven't even looked. I open it and pull out two pieces of A4 with an array of coloured post-it notes and sticky arrows. It looks like it has been assembled by a six-year-old. I begin to read.

Dear Louise and Lloyd,
Thank you so much for offering to take Marilyn on holiday with

you. I'm sure she will benefit from this wonderful life experience.
There are a few jobs that you need to do in preparation for your
trip to the passport office. The first thing you will need is to get
hold of Marilyn's birth certificate. I understand that her mother
has this. Here is her address and phone number.

At this point I break off and shout, 'Her mum lives in Yorkshire! Is effing Freda the effing Fantastic expecting me to drive to Yorkshire?'

Lloyd raises an eyebrow.

'Oh, and I need her parents' passports and birth certificates, too.'

I can feel my blood temperature rising towards 'about to explode' on the thermometer.

'And I need her grandparents' paperwork too! Lloyd, that cow has completely set us up. How the hell am I going to do all this?'

I feel like crying. It's just not possible to do it in the short space of time that we have. I'm not sure what to do.

Lloyd, ever pragmatic, suggests that I call the business manager and talk to him or her. 'See what they say and take it from there.'

I simply cannot believe that she has done this to us. My stress levels are through the roof. I can feel myself spiralling down into dark places. This is so unfair and cruel. I've put the cost of Marilyn's ticket and accommodation on my credit card already. I feel so stupid. I feel sick. What a mess.

Before I call the business manager, I call Moira. After listening to what feels like the longest recorded message in history, though I know my judgement is clouded by my frustration and impatience, I leave my voice message. 'Moira, we have a *big* problem. Call me asap.'

That should do it. I'm not going to be the only one to be on the brink of exploding because of Freda's calculated, nasty plan. How dare she leave us to pick up the pieces of the situation she has created? It isn't fair. I just can't see an answer.

Next I call the business manager, but, surprise, surprise, there is no answer and I get cut off. Terrific.

'Can you check on Marilyn to see if she needs something to eat or drink?' I ask Lloyd. 'I need to take the dogs out for a de-stress, think-walk up the fields.' It usually helps.

Once I'm in green space I let the dogs off their leads and breathe. I look across the valley and feel the anxiety lifting. This is not Marilyn's problem, poor girl. I need to keep my feelings away from her. I don't want her to feel bad. I know teenagers can act big and tough but they are children. Not only that, I suspect she has already been through a lot. Too much, probably, to bear the weight of any responsibility for this.

By nature I'm a problem-solver, and I devise a plan. I tackle what is achievable first. I will get Marilyn's photographs today. I will get double the required number to allow for any possible whoopsies. I will post the two needed by the business manager this afternoon. I am not driving all the way back to the office to drop off the pictures. Olive Freda could have told me in advance. I can't figure her out at all.

I don't know whether she is a nasty person, utterly incompetent, or just has her head in the clouds because of her imminent departure from social services. She seems too organised to be incompetent. Her goodbye to Marilyn was affectionate, so I can't believe that she's deliberately trying to be unkind. *I just don't get it.* She is hard to work out. I stop trying. It's actually beginning to fry my brain.

Back to practical plans. I think I'll call Emily, Marilyn's mum, when I get home. We're not normally allowed to do things like this without the social worker doing a 'piece of work' first. But Freda leaving with no new social worker named to take over yet leaves a vacuum.

Anyway, she gave me Emily's number and address, so it can't be that wrong, I reassure myself. Thank you, nature, I love you so much: fresh air, fields, trees and the sound of birds and sheep. I feel grounded once again and ready to sort this mess out.

When I get home, Lloyd is in the kitchen with Marilyn. I walk in and greet her first.

'Hello, sweetie.'

She beams back. She's a sweet kid really. I can see the little child beneath all the posturing and apparent maturity. A child who needs some nurture.

In my absence she has asked for chicken nuggets, hash browns and beans to eat. Lloyd is just serving up her plate.

'That looks nice. When you're finished, shall we head to the shop in town that does passport photos?'

She nods.

After she polishes off her comfort lunch she heads upstairs to do her hair and make-up.

'Do you think you could do your best to avoid looking like Trixie Mattel? Instead, could we go for "traditional office worker" for the photos?'

Marilyn laughs good-naturedly. While she goes about the business of hair and make-up, I reckon I've got at least half an hour. I decide to use the time to go into the garden and call Emily. I don't really expect her to pick up. After all, she won't know my number. So I'm caught slightly off-guard when she picks up after a few rings.

'Hello?' She has a similar voice to Marilyn; they both have a slight Essex accent.

I introduce myself as Louise, Marilyn's foster carer. She goes quiet for a second, then quietly whispers into the receiver, 'I'm going to another room.' I hear a muffled conversation and a male voice. Then, 'Hi, sorry about that. How is she?'

I explain briefly what has happened: how Marilyn arrived a few days ago and now we're going on holiday and I have to get a passport.

Emily is a little taken aback, and actually, when I consider it from her perspective, I'm not surprised.

'Right. Is she okay?' Her voice has dropped to a whisper.

'Yes, she seems fine but I only met her a few days ago, so it's still early days. We've sort of been dropped in it by her now gone social worker.'

'Freda, you mean?'

'That's the one.'

'Oh God, she's a piece of work isn't she?'

I laugh and agree heartily.

I'm surprised at her next words. 'I've been chatting to Marilyn, behind Freda's back. Marilyn swore to Freda that she would not contact me outside of any supervision, and I promised the same, but between us, I'm afraid we've ignored her.'

I actually admire their rebellion.

Emily goes on, 'Please let me contribute towards the holiday. I bet Freda suggested a bring-and-buy sale to raise a few pounds?'

I laugh again. 'Something like that, yes.'

'I always wanted to take Marilyn on holiday but, well, you know.' Her voice is sadder now, plaintive.

I can hear a man's voice in the background again. 'Who did you say that was?'

'It's Edith. We're arranging dinner.'

So she's having to lie about this to the man. That must be Alan. I keep my voice down as I explain, 'I need Marilyn's birth certificate, and yours, in order to get her passport.'

'Absolutely! I can do a chicken curry, that's no problem.

The boys like that, don't they? Lots of meat. Maybe I'll do a lamb dhansak. I know a good butcher,' she fakes a laugh.

She's a good actress. I feel like I'm in a Radio 4 play. She whispers, 'Can I have your address?'

'I'll text it to you in just a moment.'

'And bank details?'

'I don't know them off the top of my head, but I'll check and text them over in a few minutes, too.'

'Are copies okay? For the other things.'

'I'm not sure. I think I might need originals, but I'll find out.'

Suddenly she says, 'I'm thinking of the dark lace dress. I don't know if you remember the one. It's 1940s style, and very lovely. Quite tight, though, so I won't be eating much before the dinner.' She fakes another laugh.

Then I hear something in the background like 'walking the dogs.'

Emily comes back to the phone. 'Sorry about all that. My fiancé doesn't know that I'm talking to Marilyn. He's quite a stickler for the rules and he wanted me to stick to what Freda said in relation to contact.'

She pauses for a moment. 'But I can't. I don't want to. She's my baby girl.' There is a little catch in her throat. 'I love her very much. We have a strong bond, but –' She stops again. 'Well, you know,' she says, helplessly.

I do, actually.

Next I ask if I can have Marilyn's dad's birth certificate.

'Ah, well. That could be a problem. Levi lives in Australia. I'm not sure where, and I wouldn't know how to track him down. He's been there for a number of years and no longer has contact with Marilyn.' She pauses. 'Both his parents died, unfortunately. They were amazing people.'

Once again, I detect a great deal of sadness in her voice. She takes a deep breath, as if to pull herself together. 'So the honest answer is that I don't know. It's very unlikely. I can sort out mine and Marilyn's, but I don't know on her father's side.'

I ask if there are any grandparents on her side who could provide their birth certificates.

Emily is slow to respond to that. There is a long pause, almost to the point where I think we may have been cut off, or perhaps Alan has come back in. Then Emily collects herself once again. Her voice is soft, calm. 'I don't have anything to do with my family. But for the sake of Marilyn, I'll see what I can do.'

'My apologies. I must have misunderstood.' I wonder suddenly whether I read the details on the referral correctly. 'I thought your parents had looked after Marilyn?'

Emily sighs. 'They did. That's why I phone her and check up on her. I didn't want her to go there. Under any circumstances. I refused, initially. But it was taken out of my hands. The social worker made the decision.'

Oh yes, I know the feeling of things being taken out of your hands where social workers are concerned. But I don't interrupt Emily, who is in full flow.

'I had a lot going on at that time, and I was forced to go along with it. Against my better judgement. I regret it. So much.'

There's obviously a lot more to that story, but on the telephone to a virtual stranger is not the time. Suddenly I hear a loud masculine voice again. 'Emms, are you still talking to Edith? Edith, tell that bloody husband of yours to sort out some snow.'

It's the middle of summer, and so I know what that means. In my head I sing, *White lines, ahh ahh get higher, baby, get higher, baby!*

I wonder if we would all be dancing away to Grandmaster Flash if we knew then what we know now about child exploitation and County Lines. I doubt it. So, they clearly like a party.

I hear Emily say, 'I've got to go, Edith. Al needs some help with the doggies. I'll see you on Saturday at 7pm. Yes, Stan and Bev are coming. They've got their new Merc that they want to show off.' I must say Emily is very convincing.

I'm almost at the point of believing that my name is Edith and I'm a bit of a gal. I whisper, 'I'll text you later.'

'Bye, darling. Be good.'

Then that's it. I'm back to the reality of my own garden after partaking in the Radio 4 Drama of the Week. What a weird conversation. Some people's lives are seriously complicated.

I guess now would not be a good time to text, in case

Alan asks who it is and wants to see Emily's messages. I'm already becoming complicit in the deception. *Blimey, what a tangled web we weave, when first we practise to deceive!* I text Moira and ask if the birth certificates need to be the originals. Then I go and find Marilyn, who is dancing in front of the hall mirror without music. Oh Lord. How to navigate this?

'Marilyn, you look absolutely amazing, but I wonder if you can tone down some of the blusher, perhaps?'

She makes a slightly pouty face. Or perhaps a slightly poutier face, since the lipstick is doing its job.

'Maybe a little less eyebrow, and perhaps not the false lashes? You look stunning, you really do, but for the photo we need you to look easily recognisable. You can come straight back and put it back on. It's the passport protocol, not me, saying this.'

She reluctantly agrees.

Her push-up bra and cleavage are rather interesting. too. But thankfully, I think we can get away with that since it won't be in the shot. Marilyn brings down her Gucci handbag. I say 'Gucci', but it's one of those fakes you get from a knockoff market. I grab my car keys and sunglasses and head out the back to the car.

We park in one of the town's five car parks behind the post office and main shops. As we walk through the covered area to the High Street, I watch a group of lads looking at her. My first thought is, 'Back off.' My second thought is, 'Why aren't they at school?' Perhaps they're Year 11s, study leave and exams now over, who have finished the year before the rest of the students.

The photos are a success, at least after I persuade Marilyn not to do the pouty fish lips that they all seem to do in selfies these days. She sits nicely. She takes a good photo. With good bone structure and lovely cheekbones, there is no doubt that she will become a gorgeous woman, probably absolutely terrifyingly gorgeous. I get an extra set, on top of the ones for the passport and Freda's business manager. Marilyn wants to stick them to her mirror and marvel at her own loveliness. I bet starchy Freda struggled with the way Marilyn looks. This much vanity, self-love and joy wouldn't have gone down well. I'm surprised she didn't try to get Marilyn into a hairshirt whipping her own back with olive branches. But I'm sure Marilyn would look great even in a hairshirt.

When we've finished, we walk to the post office where I notice that same group of boys again. Inside, I buy an envelope and get a pen out of my bag. I go on my phone and look up the postal address for Freda's office and put Business Manager at the top, underlined. I have a notebook in my bag too. I write a little note and make sure Marilyn's name is on the back of the photos. I put it all in the envelope and go up to the desk.

I see the boys again, on bikes and scooters, hanging around outside the post office. They seem very interested in Marilyn. They're like randy alley cats. I send the photos 'recorded delivery', aware that all these little extra costs might seem small, but they are mounting up and I am unlikely to see them reimbursed. Then I get Marilyn out of the post office as quickly as I can. She has gone very quiet.

'Is everything alright?'

'Yeah, fine.'

But she isn't terribly convincing. I don't have time to follow up further. Today is about smashing through these jobs as efficiently as possible. Mission Impossible isn't going to achieve itself.

Once home, I text Emily with our address. As I do so, Moira's text appears. I don't read the whole thing, but just see *The original copies of the birth certificate* in the notification.

Of course it is. It would be. That's all I need. I add this detail into the text I have composed to Emily, intending to read the rest of Moira's text in a minute. I'm still cross with her. Almost straight away, Emily replies.

I'll put them in the post first thing in the morning. Louise, please give me your bank details.

I'm slightly hesitant, not that I think she will do anything untoward with them, but because I feel like I'm doing something wrong. On the other hand, Marilyn hasn't got a social worker for the time being, and I'm not impressed with Moira. She's staying in my bad books for now. So, while Marilyn is back in front of the hall mirror reapplying her make-up, I get my purse out of my bag and key in my bank details. I also ask for the contact details of Marilyn's grandparents, Emily's parents. Emily messages back that she will call them later and tell them to find their birth certificates. It very much sounds as if that relationship may be difficult, so I'm well aware that I must tread carefully. I need their birth certificates or I can't get the passport.

I make a mental note to message Moira again and ask her to send the business manager an email and cc me, asking for a covering letter for the passport office and for when we go away. I always have to take a letter when we travel abroad with Lily. I start to create a checklist of what I need. It's a long way to go to the passport office without the correct documents and be forced to have to go back again. I'd like to avoid that at all costs. Costs, costs, costs. They're mounting up.

Still, that's pretty much all I can do for today, or at least until Emily gets back to me about her parents. In spite of my efficiency, I'm beginning to feel stressed again. I know that the clock is ticking and I still haven't done my work. I hate feeling like this. I need my holiday. Oh, the irony!

The day has grown warmer, so when the other children get home they all raid the ice cream drawer of the freezer and run off outside. Vincent bounces his basketball around on the path. He's a big fan of the sport. Jackson sits on the bench, stabbing the seat with the scissors I left out from deadheading the roses. What is it with that boy? He can be such a caveman. Lily and Marilyn are on the old blanket on the grass. Lily has her uniform on. She wears black cycling shorts under her skirt. Such a good idea. I've got my own for when I wear skirts and dresses. Eminently sensible. Marilyn lies next to her, twiddling her hair and laughing about something. Oh, my heart sings at this level of domestic harmony. I want these friendships to continue between them when we go on holiday.

Inside, I prepare the dinner. I have recently become a greedy fan of orzo, a sort of rice-pasta. I boil it until soft, then wash off the starch in the big sieve and put it in the microwave for another four minutes. I throw it back in the pan, adding green pesto and cream, and a little dash of salt. I serve it with a salad. Today, as it's warm enough, I take their plates and the big bowl of orzo outside. They gather round and sit down to this simple but hearty meal. Vincent is a bit argumentative, but he is the youngest and still gets hangry. Who am I kidding? They all do, even me. I do some deadheading while they eat and chat about this and that. I tell Vincent off because he keeps getting up and running around, which I think is his way of trying to impress Marilyn. Marilyn's phone keeps pinging. I can't imagine it's her mum. Not that many times, over and over. She must have lots of friends, I think to myself again.

It turns from a harmonious afternoon into a nice evening. Emily texts me to say that she has spoken to her parents. *They will have the certificates ready for you if you want to go and get them. They don't want to put them in the post.* I look at the address and try to estimate the distance. Possibly a two-hour journey each way. I don't think it will be appropriate to take Marilyn, given that no family contact has been set up, and particularly in light of Emily's comments earlier.

I ask Lloyd if he is happy to look after Marilyn tomorrow, or whether he would prefer to drive to her grandparents.

'No, you go. I'm more than happy to look after Marilyn tomorrow.'

Funny that.

Still, if I leave early, I'll get the afternoon to try to do some work.

Before I go to bed I double-check that Emily's parents are expecting me. It's a long drive, so I don't want to waste my time.

Emily messages back. *They will be in until midday.*

That's great, I reply. *Can I have their number just in case I need to contact them?*

She's not keen. She suggests that I call her, then she will speak to them if I need to contact them.

I agree. What else can I do? I'll definitely make sure that Lloyd has the address so that he knows where I am. I haven't told Marilyn that I'm going to see them. I think that subject is best left alone for now. Another text pings in.

It's not you, Louise, just that my parents are a bit odd.

Okay, I think. This is going to be interesting.

VIII

Early in the morning I make sure that all the children have everything they need: clean shirts are a priority in this sweaty weather. I check on them individually before I go. When I look in on Marilyn, she's fast asleep. She sleeps with her mouth open and dribbles, bless her. She is such a baby, really, beneath the pouting and posturing and prettifying. I can hear her phone pinging though she sleeps through it.

But, hang on. I do a double-take. Her phone is downstairs. I made sure that she put it on charge down there overnight, partly as a way of ensuring that she isn't on the phone too late at night. I look across her room and realise the pinging noise is coming from somewhere underneath her bed. Before I have a chance to investigate further, she wakes up suddenly, sitting bolt upright in bed.

'Morning, Marilyn. I'm off to a meeting miles away.' Not a lie.

She nods.

'Lloyd will look after you today. Be a good girl and I'll see you later.' I blow her a kiss. She sinks back into sleep position, pulling the duvet up over her head. On the way out, I head into Lloyd's study to find that he is already on a Zoom call with clients from Europe. I catch his attention and whisper, 'I think Marilyn has another phone upstairs. Can you keep an eye, please?'

He nods.

I say goodbye and he mouths, 'Drive carefully,' at me. I kiss the heads of Dotty and Douglas and little Mabel, Lily's tabby cat. Pablo, our other, much bigger black cat jumps up on the counter and nudges my head with his. 'Wish me luck.'

They're all fed, the water bowl is full. Off I go. I feel quite the adventurer, heading out before the day has begun for most.

I double-check I have my water bottle and climb into the car. As I tap the postcode into the satnav, I wonder what strangeness today will choose to present. I listen to a bit of radio, then the inane chatter between songs begins to wind me up.

I travel for a while in silence, only the sounds of the car to keep me company. After a while, I start to wonder what all the different car sounds are, and begin to worry when I detect a change in tone.

On goes the radio once more. I used to divide my day according to Radio 4, but lately they've jiggled the programmes around and it's confused me. Good Lord, I've suddenly become a pensioner. I listen to Radio 1 for a bit and wonder if Stormzy and Ed Sheeren ever have a rest. That Taylor Swift is quite busy, too.

Eventually, after a relatively smooth ride, I arrive outside the address of Marilyn's grandparents: a semi-detached house with a pebbledash frontage. Very modest and fairly unprepossessing. There's a little pale-blue car on the drive. It's not the sort of house I'd associate with Emily and Marilyn at all, but we all come from somewhere.

The neat front garden is mostly grass with a border of depressing plants. I'm a gardener. I love plants. Somehow this looks like it belongs to someone who resents them. The doorway is arched and inside is a little porch. A plain brown doormat waits for visitors to wipe their feet. It doesn't look like a house that has many visitors, though. I notice a doorbell camera so they are probably watching me. It's a slightly uncomfortable feeling.

I press the doorbell, and within a few seconds a man appears. He was definitely watching. My first reaction is that, yes, he is rather weird. He is dressed very smartly in a pale blue shirt that's a bit too tight round the girth, and charcoal trousers topped by a black belt with a big buckle. It gives me the shivers, though I have no way to explain why. I introduce myself and stand there like a lemon when there's no sign of me being invited in.

A moment later a faded grey lady in a pale powder-blue dress appears. I notice she is wearing closed, flat, heavy shoes. Not the ideal thing on a warm day like today. She holds an envelope.

'Good morning,' she says, very formally.

I echo, 'Good morning.'

She passes the envelope to Emily's father. He holds it towards me and says, 'We want these back straight away, please.' I've met friendlier security guards with more charming rottweillers. I'm not enjoying the vibe that's coming from him at all.

'Yes, of course,' I say, ever so politely, while thinking to myself, *Really? I've got to come all the way back here?* Bloody hell.

Behind the powder-blue, I can see that the inside of their house is also frumpy. A nylon carpet, slightly shiny, runs all the way through the hall and up the stairs. The walls are painted the old NHS green, a pallid shade that was meant to be calming. There are no pictures or ornaments that I can see.

'As soon as we've sorted the passport, I'll bring back the birth certificates,' I reassure them. They don't seem at all happy about this. I guess I wouldn't want to hand my personal documents over to a stranger, either. As I put the envelope into my bag to show them that I'm keeping it safe, I notice a black attaché case and a pile of magazines: *The Watchtower*. Aaah. The penny drops. They are Jehovah's Witnesses. I know very little about this sect, only that a boy in my year at art school belonged to a Jehovah's Witness family. Pete, his name was, and it was his dad who was religious, as I recall, not his mum. He was very nice but very straight for an art student. If he lived in a house like this, I understand why. For a home dedicated to saving souls, it seems very soulless.

I get back in the car. One blessing is it certainly hasn't taken very long. Not even a cup of coffee for my trouble. But there is a bitter aftertaste nevertheless. I didn't like Emily's dad at all. He seemed fierce. He smelt, too. Of dry sweat, a horrible alpha animal smell. She, on the other hand, looked like she wouldn't say boo to a goose. Opposites attract, as the saying goes. I check the birth certificates, and to my amazement neither of them are as old as they look. He's only a few years older than me, younger than Lloyd, and she's actually a year younger than me. Jeez, life and joy certainly passed them by.

I tuck everything back in its envelope and head off with an almost involuntary shake of the head. I decide to stop off at a station to go to the loo and get the coffee that wasn't offered by Marilyn's 'charming' grandparents. I take the opportunity to check my phone. There's a message from Lloyd.

All good here. The kids got off to school fine. The sun is even shining. In other news, is it alright if Marilyn goes for a walk into town? She wants to go to Superdrug.

I text back: *Yes, that's fine. Just make sure you have her number and give her a time to be back.*

That's all good. She seems like she's settling in well. Superdrug has got lots of offers on holiday products at the moment, but I expect it's hair and make-up that Marilyn's after.

When I arrive back home, the first thing I hear is gangsta rap blaring out of Marilyn's window. In fact, I suspect anyone in the vicinity is also being treated to this music fest. Lloyd looks in agony when I go in. I laugh.

'Oh good, you're back. I don't know what she's doing.'

I dread to think, but I imagine it involves eyeliner or brow definer or some new hair product. I put the birth certificates in my room, safely tucked inside my cupboard, ready for tomorrow's long drive to Newport. I go up to see Marilyn. Her skin is orange and her hair is grey. I'm not sure if it's dye gone wrong, or if that's the look she intended. Whatever it is, it's strange.

On her bed are a whole array of new make-up trays and hair products. Wow. I tot it all up in my head. A quick calculation gives about £70 worth of cosmetics. I spy a new bottle of perfume there too. That's nearly £100. I hear her phone pinging.

'Who's that?' I ask, friendly and nonchalant.

She puts her finger to her lips 'Sshh.'

It's well played on her part because I can't ask again without sounding confrontational. She's not yet a week into her placement with us so I don't want to create any trouble, especially just before we go away.

While Marilyn dances about upstairs, I take the opportunity to check my email. Good. There's a list back from Brian, the business manager. I glance at it and see nothing scary that I've missed. Phew. That's all good. On the other hand, my stress begins to go up as I see that I need to submit two new book synopses to my agent by tomorrow. Oh God, how the hell am I going to do that? I focus and tell myself to curb the negativity and just get on with it. But after all that driving, I'm very hungry. Food first.

I call upstairs. 'Marilyn, do you want some lunch?'

'Yeah.'

A 'please' would be nice, but we can work on that later. 'What would you like?' These days children don't seem to want what I would consider typical lunch fare: a simple sandwich or a tin of soup.

'Hang on.' She comes downstairs in a very tight dress. I can't quite take the grey hair seriously. She looks like a child playing the part of a granny in the school play. She has a full face of make-up and the rest of her skin is patchy orange. I dread to think what the bathroom looks like. Never mind. I've been here before and know that streaks and spills and splotches will all wash away, especially with a little bleach.

Marilyn opens the freezer and asks for sweet potato wedges, hash browns and three eggs.

'Coming right up,' I say, cheerfully. I was thinking more along the lines of a quick sandwich, but hey. I heat up the oven and chat to Marilyn about how she got on in town and whether she found her way okay.

'Yeah, it was fine. I went for a walk around. I found the vape shop,' she says, with a raised eyebrow.

I look at her. 'No vapes, no popcorn lung and no County Lines recruitment, please, if you don't mind.'

She laughs good-humouredly.

After lunch I go back to my studio and hear the *boomph boomph* of more gangsta rap coming through the ceiling. Lovely, I think, as I rummage around looking for my Birdy CD.

Lloyd comes in after a few minutes. 'Louise, can you ask Marilyn to turn it down? I can hardly hear myself think.'

Off I go upstairs and knock on the door. 'Marilyn?'

She opens the door in another ensemble. This one is more Madame Butterfly. I ask if she can turn the volume down as we're both working.

'Sure.' She politely turns it down. Phew. That's better. I can concentrate again.

Moira calls on my mobile. My first reaction is to think, 'just ignore her, don't speak'. Then I remember to respond with my adult brain and say, 'Hello.'

I spend 15 minutes on the call to Moira, who reveals that her manager and Freda go to the same church. Aaah. That would explain Moira's total subservience.

She names the church, but to be honest, I have never heard of it before. It sounds like a made-up thing, or a breakaway wing of a more orthodox church. I find religion so confusing. It's like a supermarket where people fill their holy trolley with whatever they fancy. To the outsider, it seems strange that so many churches all say that they believe in the same God, but do it so differently. I say some of this to Moira and feel a bit like a child who didn't pay attention during that lesson at school.

'I genuinely don't understand and, after meeting Emily's parents today, I'm definitely not sold on any of it,' I say. 'The dreary clothes, for a start. What's that all about?'

I find myself chatting amicably to Moira, just as though she had not completely dropped us in it. Maybe I have embraced some Christian principles and forgiven her.

IX

I wake up with a sigh. Today is the big drive to acquire a passport. The house is quiet because everyone else is still in bed.

I've arranged as much as I can for them and hope I don't get any phone calls asking me for the whereabouts of stray sports socks or snacks while I'm travelling along the M4. I know that when I return there will be a pile of dishes that need sorting out because, even after all these years of training, entreating and cajoling, no-one apart from me appears to have figured out the mystery of the dishwasher. They still seem to think that if they pile everything on the work surface, the washing-up will somehow get done. There will also, no doubt, be an avalanche of clothes spread across the kitchen floor, and school bags scattered around the kitchen.

But it's home and I love it.

I know that it will be a good idea to check my emails to see if there are any little challenges for me to worry about before I go. Because I did a course in foster carer mindfulness and self-care, I look up directions for a nearby café and plan myself a 'care' lunch treat for when I've finished. I read an email from Business Manager Brian. He must have sent it last night, after hours. He has arranged for me to see someone at the passport office at 11am this morning, which is good because I hadn't realised that I would need to make an appointment.

I like Brian, even though we haven't actually met. He makes me feel valued and part of the team, working towards a shared end. All too often foster carers are made to feel like they don't matter. Sometimes various agencies will meet to make decisions about a child in our care and we don't even get invited because they don't regard foster carers as professionals. (Even though we are usually more experienced and know the child better than anyone.) It's a bizarre approach that makes no sense to me and is definitely not good for our morale, but Brian has helped and I appreciate his support.

Even better news – my expectations for this day are low – is that the Newport passport office is only just over two hours away. Closer than I thought. This cheers me enormously, and suddenly Mission Impossible starts to look very doable. Tom Cruise, eat your heart out.

I check the envelope again, gather all documents together, and get my keys from the pot in the hall. I check my hair and reapply my lipstick. Marilyn has turned this area into another dressing table. I shove her make-up to one side to make room for me. For a youngie she does have some very expensive products. I spot some MAC foundation, Clinique moisturiser and a Dior mascara. Fair play. She has far more quality products than I do. I notice a thin gold chain bracelet with a love heart charm dangling from the catch. I pick it up and read 'Baby Girl'.

I remember that her mum called Marilyn her 'baby girl' when we chatted on the phone. This must be from her mum. Cute. But she'll lose it if she leaves it here. I take her make-up and bracelet upstairs and quietly open her bedroom door. She is fast asleep. I tiptoe towards her dressing table and place the items down quietly, doing my best not to wake her. I turn to walk out and notice that the black Nike bag is poking out from under her bed, I push it back with my foot in case she trips over it.

Before I go, I quickly check on the others. Jackson is sleeping, snoring away with a smile on his face. Of course he is. I walk quietly up Vincent's little staircase, now followed by a mewing Mabel. Vincent is fast asleep in his lovely, tidy room. Jackson's always looks like he's been burgled by poltergeists. Lily's bedroom door is open. I think Mabel must have just done that when she heard me up and about. Now she's pestering me for breakfast. I go back to the kitchen. I'll leave the dogs for Lloyd to do or they'll run around looking for the children and wake them up too early.

The journey to Newport is, like yesterday's trip to Marilyn's grandparents' house, very straightforward. There are no traffic problems and easy parking. I wonder if government offices have an equivelant of Tripadvisor where you can leave feedback. Maybe we need a Citizenadvisor where the public can rate their local government offices on the quality of the parking, toilets and water coolers.

It's always the little things that make a difference to a day like this. How many of us go to a meeting and remember, months later, the finer detail of what was said? Conversely, how many of us go to a meeting and remember the quality of the biscuits, or the tree outside the window? I rest my case.

I check my phone and am happy to see that all is good at home. The three amigos got off to school okay. Each exit brings them a day closer to breaking up for summer, and a day closer to the holiday. I'm excited myself, but even more so because I know that they are excited. I deliberately booked the holiday dates so we can get away as soon as possible once school is out. Lloyd sends another text.

Can Marilyn go out with her friend Charlotte today, in town?

She hasn't mentioned Charlotte before. I ask who she is.

Lloyd says she's an old friend from school. That's odd. We're quite a way from where Marilyn had been going to school.

How is Charlotte getting to town to meet Marilyn?

Lloyd just does not have an inquiring mind like me. I want to know everything: the what, when, where, who and why of every situation. He gets back to me soon enough with:

Charlotte coming on the bus and Marilyn wants to meet her in town.

I reply that it's fine, *but Marilyn can bring Charlotte back to the house. I don't want two 13-year-old girls roaming around town all day.*

A few minutes later I get the confirmation. *Yep, that's fine, I look forward to hearing more Joe Grind.*

I laugh. I'm glad I won't be there for that.

I walk into the building and all goes well, apart from the fact that I will have to come back in five days to pick up the passport – the day before we fly out. Talk about cutting it fine! Oh, and the nearly £200 fee. I wasn't expecting it to be that much. On the credit card it goes. I will let Brian know and send a copy of the receipt to him. These costs are mounting up. I will max out on the card soon. I wanted to take it to Skiathos as back-up.

Because of the money I've just spent, I decide not to have lunch in a café, and instead I get a meal-deal from the nearby Tesco. I catch up with Lloyd again to ask how it's all going and find out the latest on Marilyn's adventure. She's been home with Charlotte for the past couple of hours.

Not sure if Charlotte is 13 though. She could be 20! Definitely older but nowhere near as glam as Marilyn.

Well, that last bit's hardly surprising. No-one can look as glam as Marilyn. And Lloyd isn't brilliant on ages.

Now they've gone into town to get a Costa and look around the shops for a bit, he explains in his next text. Fair enough. At least they haven't been hanging around town all day. Grabbing a drink in Costa won't take long. I head for home.

When I get back, I first check in with Lloyd, who is

on a call. He waves his hand at me: acknowledgment and dismissal simultaneously. I put my bag on a kitchen chair and pour myself a glass of water. Also, a packet of red Hula Hoops as a snack. I walk into the hall and see that Marilyn has taken over the marble-topped hall cabinet again with her make-up and hair things. I gather up the post and plonk it next to them. I walk upstairs, calling her to see where she is and if she's eaten yet. Perhaps she and Charlotte might want a late lunch.

As I approach her room I hear a phone vibrating on silent. Marilyn has left her phone on the bedside table. I end the call. That's annoying. I wanted to speak to her. I wander around the rooms, picking up towels and hanging them on the doors to dry. Jackson's bin resembles something from a film where possums have raided a house in the outback. He never opens his curtains and he leaves his light on.

I pull back the curtains and think what a shame it is that he's got such a lovely view but never looks at it. There is a trail of clothes thrown roughly in the direction of the maid's pick-up point. I'm the maid but I'm not picking this mess up. I close the door. It can wait.

I still feel a bit peckish, in spite of the crisps, and head downstairs to get my shopping bag and purse. I lean into Lloyd's office. 'I'm just popping to the shops.'

Still on his call, gives me a thumbs-up.

I give the dogs a little treat each and tell them what beautiful babies they are before jumping back in the car.

I drive to Sainsbury's to pick up some iced buns for the children. They like some carbs when they come home and perhaps that will prevent them from eating everything else in sight. As I walk across the car park I see a group of lads. I think it's the same group I saw before. I walk more slowly and clock a girl in white shorts, orange legs protruding from them.

It's Marilyn.

She's also wearing a black baseball cap with a black hoodie up over it, and sunglasses. A far cry from fitted dresses and vintage couture. There is a tall, lanky-looking girl standing next to her. That must be Charlotte. Lloyd's right: she's much older than 13. At least 16 or 17, I'd say. And she is frumpy next to Marilyn. She's in a long, baggy T-shirt over old baggy jeans and trainers.

I hang back and decide to walk the longer way round to the entrance of Sainsbury's while pretending to read my shopping list. I don't think I'd make the fieldwork division of MI5, but it will enable me to get a better picture of what's going on.

Marilyn is doing what looks to me like some Ali G moves and the boys are laughing. They're leaning against their bikes. I don't recognise the boys, which is unusual. I know most of the faces of the children in town from over the years. I don't like the look of them, I must say.

One has a buzz cut, the other two have their hoodies up and, like Marilyn, are wearing baseball caps underneath.

Marilyn and the boys have wrap-over bags slung across their fronts. Jackson would call them 'roadmen'. Apparently, there are a few gangs at school. Perhaps this is one of them. The popular kids like to hang out, look like gangsters and smoke or, as this little cohort are doing, vape. Marilyn herself isn't, I'm pleased to see, but Charlotte is vaping and looking a bit awkward. That might be because of her height, but Marilyn is the sort of girl who would no doubt make less-attractive girls feel awkward. I clock it all and go into the shop.

By the time I leave the supermarket the boys have gone. Now it's just Marilyn and Charlotte sitting on the wall, chatting. That's less of a concern. I get into the car and watch what the girls are doing. Marilyn unzips the pocket of her roadman bag, pulls out her phone and talks. Hang on, though, I know that her phone is at home. I saw it. This confirms my earlier suspicion that she has a second phone. I wait a bit longer.

Marilyn continues to sit on the wall staring at the phone, kicking her legs like a younger child. Charlotte is looking at her phone. A yellow Mini Cooper circles round and drives up to the girls. Charlotte walks up to the car and leans through the window. Marilyn pulls her cap and hoodie down over her face and looks at her phone. I don't know what to do, but I don't like this one bit. I left my own phone in my handbag at home, otherwise I would take some pictures. I watch for a bit longer. The yellow Mini drives off. Marilyn does a knuckle punch with Charlotte, who smiles. They sit back down and

Charlotte vapes again. More looking at her phone. Then, after a while, an old blue car drives into the car park. Inside are two older women, rough-looking.

The driver, who does look a fright, calls out. 'Get in 'ere.'

Charlotte, if that is indeed her name, walks over to the car and gets in the back. I can hear some effing and jeffing from the woman, who flicks her cigarette out of her window.

Their antics have drawn a few other people into watching the theatrics of the situation. Nothing like a little human drama to gather a small crowd together. I also notice that Marilyn has made herself invisible, distancing herself from the whole thing and looking on with surprise as though this is all news to her too. She is certainly a convincing little actress.

The old blue car leaves the car park. My windows are open and I can still hear shouting and swearing as they drive away. I wait a bit longer and see Marilyn getting up and making ready to walk off. She heads down the alley towards the quick route back home. If I drive around the roundabout I can pass and see if she wants a lift. By the time I get there she is already walking up the pedestrian stretch of road towards home. I'll see her at home and for now I won't let her know that I've been watching.

When Marilyn arrives home I have dinner underway and the other children are back. Vincent and Lily are in the garden. Vincent is fixing the badminton net to the trees while Lily bosses him about. Jackson is in the kitchen chopping up an onion. I ask him why and he looks thoughtful and says,

'I don't know.' We both smile, I suspect for different reasons. Lloyd lets Marilyn in. I haven't told him anything yet. If she has two inquisitors she will close down and definitely know that I know something is awry here. When she walks in she's still got her hoodie up over her baseball cap.

Jackson does a double-take. 'Roadman.'

I pretend that I haven't a clue what he's saying.

'What's a roadman?' I ask.

Marilyn does an Ali G hand thing then smiles and says, in a thick South London gangster voice, 'Alright, ain't it,' and laughs.

I ask if she's hungry.

'Yeah, man.' She swaggers around the kitchen, full gangster. She's actually quite funny. But underneath it all, I'm worried that things might not be 'alright, ain't it'.

When we're all sitting down I ask each one what they did and how their day was.

When I get to Marilyn I play the innocent. 'Oh yes, Marilyn, I hear you saw an old school friend today.'

She smiles. 'Yeah, that's right, Charlie B.'

I ask if they were in the same class at school.

Marilyn looks at Lloyd to see if he's paying any attention and he genuinely isn't; he's tucking into his dinner. Marilyn goes on to tell me that she and Charlotte have been friends since primary.

Hmm.

'Did Charlotte get the bus back home?'

'Nah, she got the bus here but her mum came and got her for the way back.'

Okay, so grains of truth here, but if they had known each other since primary school then why didn't Marilyn wave to her mum? Why does Charlotte look about 16 years old? Something isn't quite adding up.

I carry on, 'Did you have a nice day? What did you do?'

Marilyn frowns as she thinks for a second or two. 'We walked around town, went to the park, then I came back here.' She manages to leave out Sainsbury's car park which is quite convenient, but again, she hasn't exactly lied. I don't push it any further because I don't want her to close up. In my own mind, though, I resolve that Marilyn will not be going back into town for a while. I will have to think of things to do here for the next few days to occupy her. We'll have to go out to some different places or stay busy at home. I notice she is still wearing her roadman bag thing. I wonder why she's so attached to it.

After dinner they all go off and I hear the bath being run. That must be Marilyn. I've noticed that she likes a long bath, with lots of bubbles, which suits my purposes very well just now. I go upstairs and see her enter the bathroom. Once she's locked the door, I walk along to her bedroom and have a quick peek. The roadman bag is on her bed. She's taken it off, finally. I look out and double-check that the bathroom is still occupied. I can hear her music from the other side of the door, so she must have her phone with her. She has: it's gone from the bedside table. I unzip the roadman bag pocket. Nothing in there. That's odd. None of this makes much sense. But I have some uncomfortable suspicions forming. I head downstairs to update Lloyd about what I saw in the supermarket car park.

He doesn't like it one bit, either.

X

To my relief, Marilyn doesn't seem to have any particular plans for Saturday morning. She doesn't want to go out and is quite happy lounging in her room. She and Lily seem to be chatting a lot, laughing and mucking about. Marilyn is an only child, whereas Lily originally comes from a large family, and has lived here so long now that she has never been on her own. From the way she talks and carries herself, I get the impression that Marilyn has spent a lot of time around adults: not always a good thing. She has also probably spent a lot of time on her own. She is independent, and based on yesterday's antics, I get a sense that she is streetwise, probably a lot more so than we realise.

The day passes without incident. I get some work done, some more packing, some housework. But the situation with Charlotte yesterday continues to niggle away at me. Later in the afternoon I text Emily to see if she's free for a chat. She replies a little while later.

We can talk in half an hour or so. I'll call you.

When she rings, she apologises straight away. 'Sorry about that. Alan has popped out to get more wine so I can talk for a little while until he gets back.'

I tell Emily about the passport and that I have to collect it on Thursday, the day before we fly out. The tight schedule means that I'm feeling a little apprehensive. I make a little joke out of it but I hate rushing like this. Before Marilyn came I had planned and prepared everything so that on this holiday, unlike so many others in the past, I would feel relaxed and calm before I leave rather than falling asleep every 10 minutes because I'm exhausted and thereby losing the first few days. I want to enjoy it. We've earned it, and holidays do not come cheap. I don't put it quite like this to Emily, but I do tell her that I won't have time to return her parents' birth certificates to them before we go.

'So would you mind telling them for me? I'll sort it out as soon as we're back home.' I add, 'I noticed a pile of the *Watchtower* magazines in your parents' hall.'

Emily sighs audibly into the phone. 'Yes, I don't doubt it. They're Jehovah's Witnesses.'

'Oh, I see.' I don't know what else to say. There is a pause.

Emily fills it. 'It's a mad church. I hated it and I still do. I couldn't get out fast enough.'

Before I have time to say anything in response, she does that thing we all do after we've said something rude about God. 'Of course, there were *some* good people, kind people, don't get me wrong.' It comes out almost guiltily, as though she isn't quite sure if God is still listening and judging, as if she wants to leave the door slightly ajar just in case He's real. Understandable, I suppose, if you have been brought up in a climate of indoctrination.

I don't push it, though I'm keen to hear all about it. There's no time, anyhow, because she says, 'I've got to go in a minute and get ready for dinner. We have some, er, friends coming.'

I know, because I *was* Edith the last time we spoke and have a good idea what the innuendos meant. I suspect Emily and her crowd are a bit 'fruity' and cocaine is almost certainly involved, but each to their own.

'Just very quickly, then...' I ask Emily about Charlotte.

Emily has no memory of a girl called Charlotte from school. That settles that then.

'And do you give Marilyn an allowance?'

'No, social services told us not to, because Marilyn has to learn to live within her means. When we lived down south she had money, though. That's just how it is in cities: kids have money.'

Do they? I know plenty who don't have money. I wonder where it was coming from. 'Marilyn does seem to have a lot of expensive clothes.'

Emily explains to me that they've always had nice clobber. It's what they do for a living, with a shop in Portobello Road, and others dotted around the region. 'I always wanted to get involved in the fashion industry, but that had to stop when I got pregnant.'

That ties with what Marilyn herself has already told me.

'I've given Marilyn loads of clothes and have more bits for her when I eventually get to see her. Though I'm not sure when that will be. Alan's not keen and I don't drive. But I do have an original Chanel pendant that I've been saving for her. You've probably noticed already how Marilyn loves gold and bling.'

'Oh yes, I've seen the lovely engraved 'Baby Girl' chain bracelet you gave her. You know, the one with the love heart.'

There's a pause at the other end of the line. 'No, that's not from me.'

There's another pause before she says quickly, 'Look, I'd better go. I've got to shower and do my hair before they get here. I've put some money in your account, Louise. And I really do appreciate what you're doing for my daughter. Better dash, bye.' And she's gone.

I can see where Marilyn gets her high maintenance from and, I suppose, why not? Nothing wrong with a bit of self-love.

On Sunday I decide to take the children and dogs out for a drive up country, to a place where I know they will find exciting to walk. Lots of hills, and streams to jump over, a few caves. What more could a bunch of children want? While they are getting ready, I remind them to wear clothes for climbing and walking. The boys go for trainers, jeans and T-shirts, ready for action. Lily has the same size feet as me so borrows my 'proper' walking boots (that I never wear because they take too long to put on) and Marilyn is in a clingy pale grey dress with lilac edging and white trainers. Her hair is in a ponytail under a cream baseball cap, and today she has gone for a pink lipstick. She looks fabulous, no question, but perhaps more like she is lunching on a yacht in the south of France than yomping across the fields in the south of England. I do like her dress sense, though; she knows what she's doing. We all pile into the car. Marilyn sits directly behind me where I can't easily see her in the rear view mirror. I like to be able to check on them while we're driving, make sure they're okay, happy, and nobody's feeling car sick.

When we get to the woods we park up, unload the dogs, and the children pour out eagerly. Apart, that is, from Marilyn, who is still busy texting as she gets out of the car, oblivious to her surroundings. She doesn't look where she's going and steps straight into a fresh cowpat. It's not the ideal scenario for those white trainers, fake Christian Louboutins.

'It's okay, Marilyn. I can clean them up here and put them in the washing machine when we get home.' Surrounded by towels so as not to freak out the washing machine, I add to myself. Jackson and Vincent look at me and make a face.

I wink at Vincent and say, 'They're fake.'

He shakes his head. 'No, Mum. They're real.'

I look at Vincent and Jackson and they both nod in unison.

I struggle to get my head around this. 'They're over £200?'

Vincent, who is an expert on all things rap and hip hop, looks at me with a wise face. 'Nah, Mum. Think again. Those babies are about £800.'

Are they, indeed?

Marilyn walks with her hands out like little wings holding her phone. The first thing she says is, 'When are we going home?'

Alarm bells are ringing all over the place, because this is not the first thing that has bothered me. The other phone – that looks like the phone she uses most of the time. The expensive clothes and make-up, and now these pristine Christian Louboutin trainers that we definitely didn't unpack together on that first day. And now I'm also curious about that little gold 'Baby Girl' bracelet with the inscribed love heart. As I look at her, I feel a wave of panic wash over me. What is she really about? What's going on with this child? I joked about not vaping or getting involved in County Lines, because I didn't think she could be. Now I'm not sure. What is she up to? Once again, though, now is not the time.

Instead I smile and say, 'Come on, Marilyn. We're going exploring.'

She follows behind, moaning the whole time. She will not let go of her phone, even when the boys and Lily find the perfect slope for rolling down. The dogs love it too. Jackson and Vincent start at the top, lie on their sides and roll down like logs, laughing their heads off all the way. Dotty and Douglas think it's marvellous fun and try to lick their faces on the way down. I love moments like these, when it is this simple to have this much fun. Lily stands at the top calling at the boys that she can roll much faster. The dogs run back up the hill to help Lily. Marilyn, though, looks as miserable as sin. She crouches down, rocking backwards and forwards on the cowpat-encrusted trainers, biting her nails.

'Are you okay, Marilyn?' I call out.

She nods and half-smiles but looks at her phone again. I wish she'd just join in, but in her defence, the clingy dress probably isn't the best hill-rolling attire.

Lily lies down on her side and rolls down, screaming and laughing. It's hilarious. When she gets to the bottom, she pops up, brushes off the foliage and challenges the boys to another go. The three of them scramble back up the slope. Marilyn, meanwhile, is inching her way down the slope on her bottom. I watch her sadly, thinking how some children have been robbed of the simplest of childhood rights: fun and play. When she eventually reaches the bottom, the others are back up for another orchestrated tumble.

The dogs can't get enough of it, and barking and wagging their tails as if this is the most fun they've ever had. I meet Marilyn at the bottom and offer her a bottle of water. She looks pale and anxious. She stares at her phone again, biting her bottom lip.

'Marilyn, what's on your phone that's so interesting? You don't seem to be able to leave it alone. Who are you chatting to?'

She stops mid-thought and looks at me vacantly. 'No-one, nothing.'

On the way home Marilyn sits on the left-hand side, near the window, where I get a much better view. She looks ill at ease. She keeps biting that bottom lip and chewing on her nails. She glances down at her phone constantly.

Something is eating away at her.

XI

The weekend is over before I know it, and the last few days of term rattle on. I don't feel comfortable letting Marilyn go into town by herself and pull every trick in the book to prevent her going out. She has become increasingly edgy since the day of our walk. When I ask her if she is okay, she always says, 'Yeah' and either walks off or changes the subject. All her nails are bitten right down and they weren't that way when she arrived. But, in the hurly-burly of getting ready for the holiday, I put my concerns to one side. She will talk to me when she's ready.

By Tuesday evening I've packed the suitcases, and no-one is allowed to fiddle with them, 'or there will be trouble'. None of them have actually asked me what that trouble will be and I'm glad about that because, in reality, the only trouble will be for me: it will simply create more work for me to do.

As I'm closing the lid on my own suitcase, I catch a glimpse of a car parked over the road. It's a yellow Mini. Only locals park on the road, so perhaps it's a visitor for next door. I wonder who they have round. Blimey, I definitely need a holiday if this is what counts as excitement in my life. As I come back downstairs carrying some dirty washing that had been left in the approximate vicinity of the dirty washing area, I hear the front door closing. I call out, 'Lloyd?'

He's in his office.

'Have you just come in? I thought I heard the door go.'

He shakes his head. I walk to the kitchen and dump the laundry down by the washing machine. I head back out to the hall and notice that the front door is on the latch. Just as I go to close it, Marilyn walks in.

'What are you doing?' I ask.

'Nothing. I just thought I heard one of the cats outside.' This is totally credible because sometimes they are too lazy to jump over the wall and mew to be let in. I notice she's holding her phone.

Tomorrow the children break up from school. What a relief that will be, not having to rush quite as much in the mornings. The weather is okay, warmish and partially sunny, which will help get them into the summer spirit.

Because of the logistics of Thursday, when I go to collect the passport, I'm conscious that I need to have everything ready. The suitcases must be loaded into the car. With the extra space being taken up by Marilyn, not to mention her suitcase, it's going to be a bit of a squeeze. I think the boys may have to put a bag or two on their laps for the duration of the drive. The dogs are ready for their little holiday, and one of my neighbours is coming in to feed the cats. All is good. Except for Marilyn. She looks increasingly sad, or worried.

I ask her once again if she is okay.

'I'm scared.'

My mind goes into overdrive. I don't like this. The phones, the trainers, the expensive make-up, the bracelet... Is she caught up in something awful? Is she having a relationship with a much older boy, or even a man, who is giving her these things? It wouldn't surprise me, given her 'jailbait' looks. I'm not at ease at all.

Then she says, 'I'm scared about flying. What if we crash?' Her phone is in her hand again.

I ask her what she's been looking at.

She scrolls down on her phone and shows me a YouTube film about an aeroplane crash. She's been reading about deaths and accidents to do with aeroplanes.

So this is the reason she is anxious!

I sit her down with my laptop and show her some facts. I begin to wish I hadn't, since Google displays images of aeroplanes in flames, or crashed in a field or the sea. I do see one statistic that is not too frightening. 'Listen. Of every million flights, 0.06 planes crash. That's not very many. It's really low.' I compare that with road traffic crashes, reading that traffic accidents now represent the eighth leading cause of death globally, claiming more than 1.35 million lives each year, not to mention 50 million injuries.

'So what does that mean?'

'It means that we are far more likely to die in a car accident than in a plane.'

She looks at me with one of her big, beaming smiles. 'Especially if you're driving, Louise.'

I look at her and say, 'Cheeky!' and feel so relieved that a fear of flying is all that is going on. I'm still not sure about her going into town and continue to avoid letting her out before we go away. I'm not happy that Marilyn was hanging out with a much older girl and that group of unfamiliar boys. I decide that I'll take Marilyn with me to Newport, which will keep her occupied for the final morning. 'Just in case there are any issues with the passport. You never know what might crop up. I'll need to have you on hand.'

'Sure.'

At dinner, I ask the other children if any of them want to come, too. Lily thinks that's an amazing idea. The little globe-trotter is excited about going to Wales, another country, the day before we fly out to Greece.

'They don't stamp your passport when you cross the Severn Bridge, you know!'

Marilyn is pleased that Lily will be joining us. It gives her a bit of company. I can see the boys' minds working, though. Both will view us being out for the day as a wonderful opportunity to game without judgement since Lloyd will be busy working. Everyone is happy.

In spite of trip number two to Newport being another chore in a busy week, we actually have a lovely day out.

The holiday vibe has arrived and the girls have a great time. Marilyn is in tracksuit bottoms and a white cropped top. I smile and think of Sporty Spice from the Spice Girls. I wonder if Marilyn even knows who they are? Lily has borrowed Marilyn's fake Gucci bag for a bit of swag.

Before we leave, I check my emails and bank account. Moira's manager has sent me an email letting us know that Marilyn will meet her new social worker, Nancy, when we return. She even wishes us a happy holiday. I open my online account and, to my surprise, see that Emily has paid in £500. I feel a bit weird because that's a lot of money – although a drop in the ocean compared to what we've had to spend. I do hope we don't get into trouble with social services. I never quite know what the rules are for things like this but I have to say that, right now, it is very much appreciated – and needed.

I text Emily immediately to say thank you.

By the time we head to the car, Emily has texted back. *No problem, have a good time and thank you*. I'm beginning to get that holiday feeling where I start to let go and can't do much more on the home front other than get to the airport and enjoy ourselves.

Lily, suggestible as ever, is leaning into the Marilyn influence and has applied more make-up than normal, which is fine for today. She's not at school so the teachers can't tell her off, other girls can't call her a tart and boys can't tell her that she's fat. School is not always a kind place, so I'm happier when experimentation occurs outside it. That's a whole other load of issues that we are delighted to let go of for the summer. I notice that all the children relax and are happy to have a break from the social pressure as well as the academic pressure of school.

Today I see smiles and feel shared joy with the girls. I wonder how school has been for Marilyn. I noted from her referral form that she has been excluded from school in the past. But that's not particularly unusual for a child in care. To be honest, knowing that we wouldn't need to take her for this last part of term, I haven't really asked her much about her school experience to date. I tell myself there's no need for now. We can have those sorts of conversations when she's relaxed on holiday. The journey is, once again, fine. I feel I've been untypically lucky with all my driving experiences in the past week. I hope I'm not saving up all the grief for the airport run – although it's happening in the very early hours of Friday morning, so there shouldn't be any problems.

We call in at the drive-through so the girls can have some lunch. Once we get the passport, which is a matter of talking to a lovely man for just a few moments and being wished a wonderful holiday, we head home.

I might have mentally 'let go', but when I get home there still seems to be loads to do. My calm state of mind soon evaporates as I look at washing, tidying and cleaning chores that must be completed. I can't leave them while we're away. It would spoil the holiday somewhat knowing that I had to come back to mess.

I run through the checklist. We need to leave here at 2am to drive to Gatwick in good time to catch the 7am flight. I hate these very early or very late flights, but at least it means we will get the full day in Skiathos. The most important job remaining is to get the dogs round to my friend's house ready for their own little holiday. The thought of cooking this evening doesn't thrill me, so I decide to pick up fish and chips on the way home. That's one less job to worry about.

I send the children to bed at 8pm, but for once there is little complaint. Then I run around like a wild thing getting everything ready in the house for our departure. Lloyd is still sending off work right up to 10pm. We both go to sleep. Or perhaps it would be more accurate to say that we both go to bed. Lloyd does the sleeping while I lie awake worrying about every little tiny detail. At 1.30am, it's time to drag the others from their slumber and away we go.

XII

We manage to get through security without too many hitches. Vincent has put his toothbrush and toothpaste in his backpack, which means his bag slides off down the checking chute since he is carrying 'liquid' and this results in a full search. He is totally terrified. Marilyn sticks with me like glue. All her bravado has disappeared. This is all new, and she's scared and excited at the same time.

Dawn is just breaking as we walk through the winding duty-free area and reach the broad glass panes of the windows, dozens of aeroplanes lined up outside. Marilyn squeezes my arm and says, 'They're so big! Look at the size of them! They're huge! How many people do they fit on there?'

She genuinely cannot believe how big the aeroplanes are and starts looking at things on her phone – presumably the passenger capacity of a Boeing 737. Lily has been with us abroad on several holidays and the boys are seasoned travellers: they've been coming on overseas trips since they were babies. Marilyn has become like a small child. She might be three years old rather than 13, the way she is behaving. She is overwhelmed by everything. It must be a total sensory overload for her.

Of course, she cannot believe the duty-free either: all the brands, all the names, gathered together in one place. In that environment she is in a sort of heaven. She spends the £20 that Freda gave her on M&Ms and a giant Toblerone. A child in a sweetie shop. I try to explain that they might melt in the heat on the journey to the villa, but realise that nothing is sinking in.

She is so excited about the aeroplanes. She stands by the big window along with dads holding their toddlers and pointing at the sky as planes land and take off. Her delight is infectious, and rubs off a little on her foster siblings who no longer take this sheer delight in the miracle of flight.

Today is the first day that I've seen Marilyn without much make-up. I guess that 1.30am wasn't the ideal time for applying a full face of foundation, and some of what was there must have dissolved in transit. I prefer it. She actually has a lovely rose complexion that was hidden under the orange-toned base layer that she usually cakes on. She looks so young. She's just a little girl.

Our gate is already open so we walk up the corridors to get our plane. She is frightened of all the people.

'I've never seen so many people moving around in one place.' She has hold of my arm and is not letting go, although she does manage to keep checking her phone.

I glance over to see if the boys are okay. They are gently beating each other up. All good. Lily is arranging her sunglasses on her head, far more glamorous and interested in her appearance since Marilyn arrived.

We board the little shuttle bus that takes us the 50 yards or so to the plane, our bodies pressed against the doors as we drive along the ground by the runway.

I love boarding planes. My head is full of glamorous images of pop stars, film stars and famous politicians on the steps waving to the press. At the top of the steps I turn back to look at my waiting fans. The tarmac is empty. Hey ho.

Our seats are near the front of the plane. The boys dive simultaneously towards the window seat. Jackson wins, so Vincent refuses to sit next to him and goes to the row behind. Marilyn has not said a word since we reached the plane. All the new experiences piled on each other are evidently too much. She is totally silent. With Jackson in the window seat, I take the middle one, leaving Marilyn on the outside, nearest the aisle. Vincent, Lloyd and Lily fill the row of seats directly behind us.

I look at Marilyn as she avidly observes everything that's going on. She is wide-eyed, still holding on to my arm. People push past with their bags and conversation. Some wait impatiently for the aisle to clear so they can approach their seat. The plane fills with the sound and movement and general kerfuffle of passengers boarding. Overhead lockers are rearranged and their doors slammed shut.

Marilyn looks at me with a worried expression. 'Louise, it's so small. It's tiny.'

'It's like the Tardis in reverse,' I smile. It's actually very big. There are over 150 people on this plane. This fascinates Marilyn; perhaps she wasn't looking up air passenger capacities earlier. She suddenly stands up to have a look. She scans the rows of passengers behind her and then looks back at me, makes a goofy face and a 'phwoar' sound. 'Louise, there are loads of fit men on here!'

She starts laughing.

'Very funny. Now sit yourself back down before you get into trouble with the crew.'

I notice that Marilyn seems to have already caught the eye of the German air hostess. I notice, too, that the crew are a bit older than I might have expected, and I like it. They carry themselves well and have a degree of gravitas that their younger counterparts might not be able to pull off.

'Now, seatbelts.'

I help Marilyn with hers and she begins to look nervous again. I hold her hand and smile reassuringly. 'It's okay to feel a little nervous. Perfectly natural. After all, this is your first flight.'

Her right leg is shaking and this becomes more prominent as the air hostess stands in front of us to begin taking us through the emergency procedures. Marilyn squeezes my hand very hard when the crew member shows us how to add air to the life jackets. She looks at me and I see tears pouring down her cheeks.

'Louise, I'm scared. What if we crash?'

She bites her lip and looks down at her phone.

'Remember the statistics we looked at? We're not going to crash.'

'Would you mind turning your phone off now, or setting it to aeroplane mode?' the cabin crew lady asks, politely but authoritatively.

'What? What's aeroplane mode?'

'It just means turning the wi-fi off so it can't interfere with the plane radar systems,' I say, although I have no idea if that's the reason.

'No wi-fi?' Marilyn is incredulous.

The air hostess is still with us. 'Ja. That's right. Yes. Your mum is quite right. Devices must be used in aeroplane mode or with the cellular connection disabled so that signals don't interfere with critical aircraft instruments.'

Neither of us bother to explain that I am not Marilyn's mother.

'I can't-' Marilyn breaks off, biting her lip.

'They're addicted to their phones,' I smile at the hostess. 'Just turn it off, Marilyn. You heard the lady.'

Soon enough the sound of the engines starts up. Marilyn looks at me in alarm. The sound indicates that we might start moving soon, and the proximity of take-off seems to freak Marilyn out further.

'What if we crash? I can't do this!'

Some old training course advice comes to the forefront of my mind from somewhere in the dark recesses of my brain: *never promise anyone that everything will 'be okay'*. I've always struggled with this as an approach since my natural response to anything bad is to reassure people and say, 'it's okay, it'll be alright.'

I suspect that the reason we are encouraged not to offer our naturally soothing response of 'it'll be alright' is down to insurance. If in an official capacity as a foster carer, and perhaps even in other walks of professional life – social worker, teacher, paramedic, say – you reassure someone that 'it'll be okay' and it isn't, then no doubt, in our litigious culture, you could be in legal trouble.

Marilyn is scared though. Really scared. I can feel her fearful breath on my face. I continue to hold her hand. She wants to wriggle out from the seat, even though we aren't even airborne.

She pulls the magazines from the pocket in front as she leans forward in an attempt to escape from her seat, forgetting that she is securely strapped in and the seatbelt signs are on ready for take-off. I try to pull her back and shout in a whisper for her to calm down. She grabs my bare arm so tightly her fingernails draw blood.

The air hostess throws us a look that terrifies me. I can see the other hostess, who was getting ready to settle herself into the jumpseat, stand up and shift calmly into action.

Marilyn screams, 'I want to get off! Get me out!'

I feel myself burn with the shame. Shame that I am just her foster carer, not her mum. Shame that we are causing this scene and disturbance. Shame that half the plane is watching and who's to say they all feel calm about flying anyway? Jackson looks at me, a panicked expression on his face, reflecting my own helplessness.

'Stay calm,' I say. 'It's okay. It'll be alright.'

Marilyn is now talking very fast, very loudly, 'Let me out, let me out of here!'

The air hostess who was doing the safety talk rushes through the last few seconds of it.

Marilyn has by now undone her belt and is wrestling out of her seat, whacking me in the face as she grabs and pulls at anything and everything. She is terrified. This is pure white fear.

The air hostess throws down her props and rushes towards us. Marilyn is screaming now. 'Let me out! I'm going to die!'

Lloyd leans over the seat to pat my shoulder as reassuringly as it is possible to do through the small gap between chairs. He notices the blood on my arm and the bruise on my cheek that is already turning blue. 'That's going to look beautiful on the beach,' he jokes.

'You're not helping.'

It takes two cabin crew to calm Marilyn down. While one holds her hands to stop her thrashing around and hurting herself, the other strokes Marilyn's hair and asks her gently if she's ready to sit back down.

After about five minutes (which felt like five hours), the two women lift Marilyn gently back into her seat. The next bit is amazing.

The air hostess who did the safety presentation calmly stands to address the plane. 'Ladies and gentlemen, boys and girls, we have experienced a young girl in distress. I ask you to delete any film or photographs you may have made of her distress and I ask you all to sit back down. I remind you that the seat belt signs are on as we will shortly begin taxiing out to the the runway. We should be able to make up the time on our journey. So now, I would ask you to allow our young passenger the dignity and respect that she deserves and put the incident from your minds. Thank you for your cooperation.' The words have even more power with her thick German accent. I want to give her a standing ovation. What a brilliant woman.

But it's an inauspicious start to the holiday, and we haven't even taken off yet.

XIII

Marilyn is worn out from her collywobbles. After some 'on the house' snacks from the magnificent cabin crew, she snuggles up into my arm and side as comfortably as she can once I've moved the armrest out of the way and falls asleep.

Throughout the flight, the staff continue to check on Marilyn and our family. When we eventually touch down and are ready to disembark, Marilyn goes in for a big hug with her saviours and I cry – which is rather annoying since, by the time we get to passport control, I feel 104 years old.

I was so busy before we left that I didn't get a chance to do my usual pre-holiday beauty treatments. I'm in need of a good pedicure. My toenails are chipped, and they're normally perfect when we go away. Once I even had gold leaf appliqued on them. I haven't done a face pack and my hair is all over the place. I feel so, so tired, and now demoralised. I think of pious Freda the Fearsome in her olive ensemble, cool as a cucumber, while I feel and look like a sack of potatoes. With a big bruise on the cheek. Right now, I hate my life!

We stand by the luggage carousel.

Marilyn weeps and splutters. 'I want to go home. I hate it here.'

The children are standing as far away from her as they can without getting back on a plane. Lloyd is doing his best to keep them amused but I am physically and mentally exhausted. I'm absolutely hanging. I feel one inch away from saying, 'Oh shut up and pull yourself together. You're on holiday.' But I know only too well that, in the words of an old professor friend, 'that'll go down like a shit sandwich'. So I do what so many mothers and foster mums have done before me. I sigh, think of the large gin and tonic I shall soon be sipping and instead say, 'We'll soon be at the villa.'

'Vill*as*,' Lloyd reminds me.

We have a pre-ordered taxi. The driver is a large sweaty man who looks disapprovingly at Marilyn. To be fair, by now she resembles a rag doll. The children maintain their excitement but have told me at least 50 times that they are hungry. Poor flowers. I am parched, dispirited and dead on my feet.

Marilyn is still pleading to go home as we whizz around tight village lanes with suitcases on our laps. The driver seems first surprised and then cross that six people on holiday from England for two weeks brought suitcases with them.

Finally, we get to the villas. We pay the taxi man, and I mutter something rude under my breath that I wouldn't dream of repeating but somehow, and in spite of his poor

English, he hears and understands me. There is an awkward moment, but frankly, right now, I'm growing used to them.

We find someone to check us in. It's a family-run business, the family consisting of the mother, father and two grown-up children. I note that mum is cleaning, dad is out and the daughter, Persephone, is running around doing everything while the son is sitting down with a cold drink watching the TV. I hope Jackson and Vincent don't get any ideas about the gender stereotypes I've worked so hard to break. If they do, I will quash them – especially given the mood I'm in right now. I ache with tiredness and stress. Persephone signs us in and takes our credit card details. She explains that because of our short notice to change the accommodation, they couldn't give us the villa next door. Lloyd and myself are in another villa one door up.

My heart sinks.

This lot in a villa, without an adult, with a kitchen and electrical things. I don't think so. We all pick up our suitcases from where the taxi driver dumped them and walk them through a side path. All, that is, apart from Marilyn, who is standing by the reception area looking at her phone, while hugging herself.

I say, rather sharply, 'Marilyn, you need to bring your suitcase. Please pick it up.'

She looks at me murderously. 'No. Why should I?'

My stress levels are rising by the minute.

I go back and get her suitcase. It's easier than arguing.

Frankly, I do not feel like engaging in any conversation about the rights and wrongs of this situation and her response to it. With the keys, we head firstly to their villa. It's nice and we would have all been in here together if it hadn't been for bloody Freda.

Marilyn bags the big double bed on the mezzanine. The others are avoiding her, perhaps unsurprisingly, so opt to create their own dormitory downstairs. I feel very ill at ease leaving this lot alone. I laugh to myself because in a social work panel session not so long ago we were told by the Chair of the panel that she did not allow foster children to sleep in double beds. She gave no rationale, but that was her rule. If she was worried about sexual abuse, that alone would have revealed a complete lack of understanding: sexual abuse can happen anywhere. I have only ever known children to love the opportunity of a double bed.

Still, what can I do? This is out of my hands. We get them settled. Vincent loves the fact that they have doors into their own private garden. Rather bemusingly, he is thrilled that they have their own washing line. Bizarre. But then again, I suppose these things are the little leaks of independence from their futures.

We leave them to unpack. I laugh again to myself as I can guess what their 'unpacking' will look like.. Lloyd and I head over to our villa. It's much smaller than theirs, with just the one bedroom, but still very nice. We don't have a garden like the big villa. Instead we have a balcony. I stand on it and look at the view: green hills and cypress trees. I take a deep breath.

I feel rancid. I didn't know it was possible to feel this tired and disheartened when you were supposed to be on holiday. And it's only day one.

I tell myself to snap out of it. I am a great believer in stopping self-pity and getting on with it. Feeling sorry for yourself is not helpful here, Louise. I am an adult and responsible for four children and, even though I'm tired as hell, I am the adult. I am not the only adult: I have support from my fellow adult, Lloyd. Who has put his bathing trunks on his head and is singing the falsetto bit from Bohemian Rhapsody with great gusto. Well, perhaps I am the only adult on this holiday.

I have a shower and immediately begin to feel much better. My stomach is gurgling so it's definitely time to eat. It's too early for lunch, but by the time we get them ready to head down to the beach and locate the lovely-looking tavernas shown on the website, it will most definitely be lunchtime. I feel more human and put on one of my summer dresses. It's one that I never wear in England, the sort of dress that if you stand in the light you can see through it, but here I'm just not fussed, because I don't know anyone and anyway, no one cares.

I look down at the disgraceful state of my toes and vow that this will never happen again. I never go on holiday or wear summer sandals without a pedicure and polish. It's a small thing, I realise that, but it's exacerbating my feelings of dismay. I'll get some stuff from the shop and sort myself out. That will make me feel better. But first, food! I go into the bedroom and find Lloyd sound asleep on the bed. Brilliant. I tap his leg and say, 'Lloyd. Lunchtime.'

He wakes immediately. We go and gather the children. As predicted, Marilyn has put a few clothes away, then got bored. Jackson has basically tipped his suitcase out on to the floor. Lily has packed most of her clothes away in drawers and set up two teddy bears on her bed. I didn't know they were coming. Then I realise she isn't the only one. Each of the children has brought a teddy. How interesting. Even Marilyn. I haven't seen hers before. It's a grey fluffy teddy holding a big red heart saying 'I love you'.

Unlike the adults, the children all seem in reasonable shape and are begging me for food. I check the kitchen to make sure they haven't played with the cooker and hob and we all head out. The little snack bar by the pool doesn't seem to be open, nor are there any villa residents in the pool itself. It looks quite inviting, though.

'Let's head to the pool when we get back,' I suggest.

We bypass the tavernas and find a restaurant by the beach that does a selection of pasta dishes. While I'm anxious to sample some traditional Greek fare, the reality is that we all need something stodgy to fill us up. A carbohydrate festival is what is required. Pasta and bread. We're all dehydrated too. The waiter takes our order. Starters and mains. We mean business. Marilyn is not the most adventurous eater I have met, so we order chips and some fish, and a basket of bread.

She's put her hair into a high ponytail which, with the lack of make-up, presents a much younger Marilyn. She holds her phone the whole time, only putting it down to eat. She is inseparable from that thing. I think we're going to have to implement some mobile phone rules if it carries on.

The children's energy soon picks up, as does mine and Lloyd's, once the food hits the spot. After we pay the bill we go for a first look at the beach. I buy the children ice creams as a treat. It finally starts to feel like a holiday. Until we walk on and suddenly hear screaming.

We turn around to see where the screaming is coming from. It's Marilyn, freaking out because a wasp has flown near her.

I look at Lloyd, exasperated.

He shrugs, and takes over, realising that I don't have an ounce of patience left. 'It's okay, Marilyn. It's fine. If you stay calm and leave the wasp alone, the wasp will leave you alone.'

That doesn't seem to resonate with Marilyn, who keeps on screaming and waving her phone hand in the air.

People are beginning to watch this extraordinary sight. It is just one wasp and Marilyn, but the wasp will not go away. It just keeps on flying around her. It's as if it is and enjoying the show.

I walk back to her and take the ice cream out of her

sticky hand. I pull a tissue from my bag and say, 'Rinse your hand in the sea.'

When she comes back I have wrapped the tissue around the cone to keep her hand free of sugary drips. I give her another tissue and say, 'Wipe your face. It's covered in sugar and the wasps think you've invited them to lunch.'

It's these little things that remind me that not all children, or indeed their parents, understand the most basic and practical aspects of parenting.

We walk back to the villas and I suggest we all hang by the pool for the rest of the afternoon until it's time to get ready for dinner. Oh, I love holiday life. It's amazing. I love the meander from one meal to the next, knowing that I'm not going to be the one making it, or doing the clearing up.

The children all go back to 'their' villa, and I realise that I'm just not going to ever be happy about this accommodation divide. It's wrong. *Grrrr*. That bloody Freda. I don't think I can forgive her for this.

A few minutes later, having grabbed a towel, I head back over to meet everyone by the pool. I plonk my bag down on a sun lounger, catch sight of my chipped toe polish and remember that I need to buy some varnish remover and polish. It's really bothering me that I have not got nice toes! It feels like a tiny, but significant, loss of self. They look like the feet of a stranger, and I don't want to be responsible for them. I always have nice toes for sunshine. This is the first time…

Watch it, Louise! I pull myself back in before I spiral into that depressive loop. I know I'm behaving like a stroppy teenager. Perhaps it's being surrounded by them that's doing it. Sulking isn't a good look, especially for an adult. I also remind myself that it isn't going to achieve anything other than encourage me to wallow in my own misery. I line up five more sun loungers and settle myself down.

One by one, the children appear. Jackson and Vincent run along the side of the pool then dive bomb in. Right behind them is a notice that says no diving. I will explain this to them in a minute. Here comes Marilyn: white Speedo swimsuit and white Adidas shorts, hair up and huge sunglasses, the look complete with her little fake Gucci bag. She is barefoot and her toenails look great, adding to my shame. Of course, she is holding her phone. I'm beginning to think it must be superglued to her fingers.

Last but not least, is Lily. Lily is in a swimsuit and hoodie, flower pot hat and carrying a new beach bag, a book and a bottle of water. Still no sign of Lloyd.

The boys love the pool. They are in their element, leaping around, making a game out of everything. Lily settles herself down beneath a palm tree, looking ready for some serious relaxation. Marilyn is under her towel, looking scared. Perhaps she fears another wasp attack. Who knows?

'Right, you two. Put some suntan lotion on.'

They do so, but Marilyn is ill at ease, unable to settle.

Lord knows where Lloyd is. I don't want to leave the children alone in the pool so I just hope that Lloyd will show up soon. He can't have got lost. The layout of the villa complex is very straightforward.

The afternoon evaporates in sun and water. The boys mess about incessantly and laugh themselves silly. Lily is in and out, swimming to cool off every quarter of an hour or so as she gets too hot. She goes to the other end of the pool to avoid being splashed by the boys.

My mind wanders. I have a memory of when I was an artist in residence at a primary school, years ago. I noticed how the boys occupied all the space in the middle of the playground. I remember thinking how wrong it was that the girls were brushed to the edges. I call out to the boys, 'Let Lily have some space, please'.

I watch Marilyn as she fidgets away, still holding the phone as if it's a comforter. She is really ill at ease.

'How are you doing, Marilyn?' I ask. 'Are you okay?'

She looks at me. 'No, I'm not. When will I go brown? Why aren't I tanned?'

'Love, it takes more than five minutes to tan, and you need to be careful. Tanning is an art that has to be done slowly, in stages, otherwise you'll burn. You have beautiful skin and you'll have a healthy glow in no time. Relax and enjoy it.'

She huffs and lays back down on the lounger. I keep an eye on everyone's skin to make sure nobody is going pink. It's easily done on day one, and I don't want anyone's holiday ruined by sunburn.

It's not long before tummies are rumbling once more. I walk back with the children and ask them all to get ready for dinner.

'You have an hour. Be sensible about showers and bathroom time.'

Vincent has found a music channel on the widescreen TV and says he is nearly ready.

I beg to differ. 'Um. It looks very much to me like you're still in your swim shorts.'

'Chill! We're on holiday.'

I leave them to it and head into our little villa. Lloyd is fast asleep. I might have guessed. He could sleep on a washing line if he had to. He's always been able to fall asleep anywhere and I sometimes wonder if he has a mild form of narcolepsy. I, by contrast, am too busy being hyper-alert and vigilant to be able to do that. All sorts of reasons for that, like fear of being murdered. And when you have children, it's hard to settle until they are asleep – although Lloyd doesn't seem to suffer with this particular affliction.

I wake him up, slightly resentfully, as he has been snoozing and I would love to. Even though I have been 'relaxing', I've been watching the children like a hawk all afternoon. And, given the early start and my insomnia the night before, I'm feeling decidedly lacking in sleep. I have that gritty feeling behind my eyelids.

We get showered and ready to go out. We head over to the 'young' villa to collect the children who, I must say, have all made an effort this evening. Marilyn looks completely overdone, almost as if she was a man in drag, but hey, it's her show.

We walk down the many steps to the road and head towards the beach, where people are milling about and the smell of the restaurants is tantalising. We find one that faces the sea. I order beers for me and Lloyd, and then almost straight away another round, as I am parched and on holiday.

Marilyn is behaving strangely. 'I don't know if I can sit here. There are wasps.'

There aren't, but it's the time of day when other little creatures might be flying about so we ask the waitress if we can have a yellow insect candle. She brings it over. We are all tucking into our starters when Marilyn suddenly jumps up and starts screaming. She knocks into the people sitting next to us who are polite, but clearly annoyed. Marilyn runs out of the restaurant towards the beach, screaming and shouting.

'I'm going to die,' she shrieks.

I take a deep breath and watch my dinner arrive at the table as I leave the restaurant in search of Marilyn.

XIV

Last night I sat in with the children until they went to bed, and then stayed up waiting until I thought that they were all safely asleep. It still feels wrong that they are all underage and in a different villa. I know that Jackson and Vincent are responsible, and Lily too for that matter. Still, I can't help feeling concerned for their safety. Amazingly, even nice Brian didn't want to do a risk assessment of the holiday. If we were at home I would have to run everything past them – sleeping in a double bed, even having their hair cut – but once we are out of the country they don't seem to give a hoot.

My friend, who has a static caravan near Bournemouth, has to do a risk assessment every time she takes the foster children there. She has to do a virtual tour of the site and send it, everything. Partly because she fosters, she can't afford to take all the children anywhere else on holiday. She's an amazing woman but, in my opinion, easily taken advantage of because of her innate goodness.

Our society sees human kindness as weakness. I make a

mental note to have a strong word with her when I get back. She needs a break too.

Which, I remind myself, is what this two-week holiday was meant to be for me. And yet, on day two, I'm still so tired my eyelids ache. Perhaps I'm the one that someone needs to have a stern word with: after all, I've somehow been persuaded to take a child I've barely met away on our family holiday.

The plan today is that we will once more head off to the beach in plenty of time to get a good spot. It's amazing how much earlier the children seem to wake up on holiday – when they go to bed later and when there is all the time in the world to relax and sleep in.

I also want to find a supermarket. We can't afford breakfast, lunch and dinner out every day, especially not with one extra at every meal. If I get some bits and pieces this morning, I can cook food in their villa and leave them with plenty of snacks. I think tonight I will cook pasta and make a salad. I love the giant tomatoes here.

They also need to make their own breakfasts. I will just have to live with the fact that I will have to clean up after them.

Lloyd is up and smiling. I'm not surprised. He has had tonnes of sleep. I think I've had about four hours in three days. I feel grubby. That's how severe lack of sleep makes you feel. And I must sort out my toes. I keep thinking about it, but I still haven't done anything about it. Every time I look at my feet I feel like a failure.

The poolside snack bar is open. The opening times seem

pretty random. I'll ask to see when they are officially open and closed. We all have toasted sandwiches for breakfast. That will keep them going until we get to the beach. I saw that one of the shops did cheese and ham rolls. I'll get six of those plus loads of crisps and fruit, and litres and litres of water. They must stay hydrated and I'm not sure any of us drank enough water yesterday.

Getting to the beach takes a little longer than anticipated, partly due to my quick lunch shop, but mostly due to Lloyd spending a small fortune on lilos: two crocodiles, one donut with a bite taken out of it, and a watermelon; and then having to wait while they are blown up in the shop. After that there is the business of negotiating how to carry them between us.

Marilyn is made to carry her own beach bag and lilo, which doesn't go down very well. I might as well have asked her to carry a poo bag full of Dotty's business down to the beach. I'm beginning to feel like her servant. She is a bit of a prima donna. I can't think why I didn't notice it so much at home. Probably because she barely had time to settle in and reveal her true colours.

Once on the beach, though, Marilyn is so excited as we wade through sun loungers and parasols. She looks at me (with a face that is fully made-up, totally unsuitable for the beach) and gasps, 'It's like a film!'

There are bodies everywhere, all shapes and sizes, all different colours. You can spot the English people a mile off.

They always appear to be the ones who are a little on the red side. I resolve once more that no-one is going to get sunburnt on my watch. I show them where they can set up camp and slather suntan cream, factor 50, all over them. They actually look very white. Marilyn has pale skin, but she does look like she'll get a nice golden tan if she does it properly.

The boys slap theirs on as if there is no time to lose. They dump their stuff and run into the sea, powering down as if they are entering the water at the start of a triathlon.

'Chill!' I call after Vincent, tongue firmly in cheek.

Lily hangs back for Marilyn, who is standing up, still wearing a tight T-shirt dress. Lily has advised her to wear her swimsuit underneath for ease of changing, but she is reluctant to strip off. We manage to lure Marilyn to the edge of the water. She dips her toes in but hangs onto my arm, a bit like when we were on the plane. My arm is still sore from where her nails tore into it. She keeps looking at me and giggling at the rushing waves. Again, I'm struck by how much of a little child she is, despite the make-up (which is rapidly melting and fading in the heat and sea spray).

Lily has no such qualms and plunges in for a swim. When she comes out of the sea she asks Marilyn if she would like to go right in.

'Um, not at the moment.' Marilyn decides that she is not going to take her dress off. In spite of the figure-hugging outfits, she is actually very modest in some ways, and clearly does not feel comfortable about being in her swimsuit in public. There is a degree of insecurity here. I have memories of feeling embarrassed as a young woman too.

I don't say anything, though. I watch Lloyd look perplexed at Marilyn's reluctance to take her dress off. I throw him a look that says, 'Do not say a word'. I sit down on my towel, happy in my swimsuit. Frankly, I no longer care what anyone thinks of me or my body. (I just hope that no-one judges my toes.) Lloyd sits next to me on his towel and we watch the children at the shoreline. I put some rocks on the lilos as there is a bit of a breeze.

Marilyn stands in the sea up to her knees with the rest of her dress bone-dry. She is still holding her phone. Part of me wishes she'd drop it in the water.

Suddenly, Marilyn's arms start to flail and she begins screaming, 'Wasps!'

What a sight she looks, standing in the water waving her arms about, shouting her head off. I notice the boys look at her, say something to each other, and move further up the beach to distance themselves from the spectacle. Lily looks at us for support, by which time I am standing at the water's edge, calling Marilyn to come back to the towels.

Her face is a mess. Black mascara has run down her cheeks. She walks quickly towards me and grabs my hand. I lead her back to the towels. She takes the boys' towels and wraps them around herself. She sits with her arms around her knees, still holding the phone, shivering and pleading to go back to the villa.

'But we've only just got here.'

Her bottom lip is quivering. I know this will sound harsh to a reader, but it's so pronounced that I'm convinced it's fake.

I look to my left and my right. People are looking at us – or should I say at Marilyn. My shoulders slump in defeat. 'I'd better take her back,' I say to Lloyd, then whisper, 'Or she'll ruin it for the others.'

I take a deep breath. 'Right then, Marilyn. We'll walk back to the villa.'

She instantly stops shivering and starts gathering up her bits and pieces, including her watermelon lilo, as yet untested. As we make our way to the boardwalk that leads to the alley through the restaurants, we pass a group of older women lying on towels and loungers, chatting and snoozing. They are topless. Marilyn suddenly stands still and throws her bag down. Initially I just assume that she's fed up with carrying it and is having a tantrum in the hope I will carry it for her.

She could just ask, we don't need the drama about a beach bag, do we? I think, rather uncharitably.

Then suddenly she shouts, 'Eeeew, that's disgusting!'

I look around and wonder if she has stepped in something stinky. Before I get the chance to say anything she is standing, holding the phone, waving her arms around, shouting, 'That's disgusting! Why have they got their nasty , sagging tits out? I feel sick!'

My blood has risen and I am half-humiliated, half-raging. I move towards her, wishing, as I have done on so many other occasions during my time as a foster carer, that I had a sign to pull out that says *Sorry, please forgive. She is my foster child. We're doing our best.*

I snatch up her bag and grab her by the wrist. One of the women says something which I think might be in German. They might not be speaking English, but from their demeanour, they clearly understood what Marilyn has just said. They sit up, look at her expectantly, then, when she says nothing else, look back at me.

'I am so sorry,' I say.

They are decidedly unimpressed.

'You are beautiful women,' I say, mustering all the honesty I can. 'She hasn't seen such naturally confident women before. Please accept my apologies. You look great. You really do.'

A nearby couple, clearly English, are killing themselves laughing. I blow out an exasperated sigh. They laugh even more. None of this is helping.

I march Marilyn through the alleyway in the direction of the supermarket. I'm on holiday, I'm exhausted and I'm stressed. I'm getting myself a cold lager and some snacks. Then I'm going to sit by the pool and she can, frankly, do whatever. Once out of the shop, when I've calmed down a little, I ask Marilyn, 'What was going on with you back there?'

'What do you mean? They have saggy old boobs. They should cover 'em up.'

I tell her they can do what the hell they want, their bodies are their own. 'And they are tourists. Guests on holiday, just like us. Trying to relax and have a good time! Just try to remember that.'

She bites her nails and looks at her phone. I realise I am carrying her bag.

'Moreover, young lady, this is yours and you can carry it for yourself.'

She ignores me.

I drop the bag on the floor and walk off.

'Louise, you can't do that!'

I reply, 'I just did,' and keep walking up the lane back to the villas.

She follows, trying to keep up with her bag and lilo. I can hear the sound of her flip flops flicking against her heels with each step.

Right now, I do not know what to do or think. She is being outrageous. I know that all this is because she is totally out of her comfort zone and ultimately feels unsafe, but now I feel unsafe too. I can't take her anywhere. She's rude, she's a liability, she's quite capable of getting us into who knows what sort of trouble, and that damn phone is annoying the hell out of me!

I climb the steps to the villa door, at which point I realise Lloyd has the children's keys. Terrific. So I carry on walking to the pool.

There are a few people sitting quietly by the pool, enjoying their day in perfect peace, and here we are, coming along to ruin it. I've left our lunch at the beach so order us both a toasted sandwich – not a varied diet so far this holiday – and some drinks. I walk to my lounger and, in the absence of a fridge, tuck my ice cold can of lager underneath to keep cool while I eat lunch.

After a moment I notice Persephone staring at Marilyn, who does look a mess, I have to say. She leans under the counter and produces a packet of wet wipes. She pulls a few out and says, 'For her face, her eyes.'

'Ah, thank you. That is kind.'

It is kind. Marilyn resembles a low-budget Widow Twankey.

I sit back down and suggest Marilyn does too. We eat our lunch and I drink the lager. I have half a glass and in my tired and stressed state, start to doze off in the sunshine. I'm woken by screaming. Marilyn is running around the perimeter of the pool, stooped over, holding her phone. It's the wasps again, apparently, but I can't see any.

An Englishman and his family are watching her.

I call out, 'Marilyn, that'll do. There aren't any wasps.'

She insists that she is being followed by one.

I say again, more firmly, 'Marilyn, there are no wasps. Come and sit down please'.

She runs up to me and shouts, 'Fuck off, Louise. You're such a bitch. I'm going to my villa.'

The man stands up and calls out, 'Oi! You need to keep her under control.'

It sounds like he's referring to an untrained pooch. I feel defeated.

Within a few minutes, she is back. 'Where's the key?'

Very calmly, I explain, 'Lloyd has the key.'

'Go and get it then.'

Oh, I am so fed up. My response is simple. 'No.'

She paces up and down, shouting. My head aches. My body aches. I feel like I'm in a mini hell. The man gets back up. He's heading towards me. Oh God, this is all I need.

He leans in towards me. 'Has she got special needs?'

I am grateful that he hasn't shouted at me. 'She's our foster child. She arrived two weeks ago and now we're here.' I shrug.

'Oh, wow. That's terrible. What? They let you bring a new foster child on holiday?'

Put like that, it does sound ridiculous. I feel as if I may have found an ally. I correct him, politely. 'It wasn't so much let, as insist. It was never our plan. We were pushed into it.'

He goes on to tell me that his sister used to foster. 'What a bloody nightmare that was. Her husband left because it was so bad.' He pauses, then to my surprise says, 'Good on ya, though. I admire you. Can I get you another drink?'

I look down and see that mine has been knocked over, presumably during Marilyn's Flight of the Invisible Wasp performance around the pool.

'That's kind. Thank you.'

He comes back a few minutes later with a fresh beer.

'And I know you know this, but if you ignore her, she'll calm down.' Then he winks at me.

I sit with my drink, staring at my chipped toenail polish, which now seems symbolic of my current mental state. I take my sunglasses off and use them as a mirror to see if I can work out where Marilyn has got to. She is sitting on the wall behind me, looking at her phone. By golly, he's right!

Lloyd comes back with the children and a few carrier bags of food. Excellent, he's done the shopping for this evening. Good on him. I'm grateful. Still, he's had a perfectly nice day at the beach and not had to deal with Marilyn and her deeply unpleasant comments and outbursts.

'Don't suppose you picked up any nail varnish?'

I rummage in the bags as he plonks them down next to me and ascertain that, basically, it's chocolate and crisps. No, wait. There are some onions, a whole garlic bulb and some pasta, plus lots of my favourite big tomatoes whose skins are just beginning to split from their time in the sun.

'No. Did you ask me to?'

'No.'

'And I'm not telepathic, so –'

Fair enough.

Marilyn is still sitting on the wall. I have been keeping an eye on her as best I can. No more snoozing for me. Lloyd pulls the keys out of his pocket and gives them to Jackson. The children head into their villa, where Vincent immediately turns on the music channel and starts singing to some rap music. Lily dumps her bag outside and says she's having a shower. Jackson, who is evidently loving the domestic independence, puts the various chocolate-related food items in the cupboards. He puts the crisps on the side.

'What time is dinner?'

I look at my phone. 'Around 7pm.' Which is in an hour and a half.

He takes that as an invitation to open one of the giant packets of Cheeto crisps and sits in the garden munching on them, loving life.

Marilyn drags herself onto her bed and looks at her phone.

I tell them I will call them all for dinner at 7pm.

I persuade Lloyd to cook, since that can of lager has made me even more sleepy. I feel shattered. He makes a big pan of pasta and sauce. I make a salad and cut up a stick of bread. We head to the children's villa where we can sit out in the garden.

I try to ignore the mess in the young villa, clothes everywhere. Vincent's room, however, is not a mess. His clothes are all packed away neatly, his suitcase is under his bed and he is very chilled.

Marilyn joins us. 'Would you like to eat yours indoors?' I ask her.

She agrees and I feel relieved. It's not very sociable, but at least this way we won't have to suffer her 'wasp' antics. I need a quiet evening. I feel so tired that I ask Lloyd to sit with them while I go to bed. I also remind them that between them they can do the washing-up. Because they regard this as their house and they have some pride in it, Lily and Jackson sort it all out while Vincent hangs the wet towels on the washing line. It's a miracle.

I go to our villa and lie down on the bed, switching the television on. I have no idea what I'm watching; it looks like a soap opera but it's all Greek to me. It doesn't take long until I'm asleep. Lloyd comes in at about 11pm.

'I sat up with the children playing games and watching films until they decided to sit in bed with their iPads and phones,' he explains when I stir. I hate them being in another villa, I really do. It has complicated everything.

Lloyd has bought new batteries for the fire alarms. That puts my mind at ease a little. He makes a cup of tea and lies down on the bed next to me. I notice that his feet are red.

'You need to put sunscreen on your feet,' I tell him automatically, slurring in my drowsiness. I drift off back to sleep.

Bang! Bang! Bang!

A manic, bailiff's knock.

'Good God, what's that?' I say, instantly awake. I jump out of bed and open the door. It's Jackson, Lily and Vincent. They pile in, bordering on hysterical.

'Quick, quick. You've got to come quick. Marilyn is trying to kill herself.'

'She's got a blade!'

'There's blood everywhere.'

I'm in emergency mode, in control. 'Stay here.'

I race to their villa. I walk in and call out, 'Marilyn?'

I can hear crying. I go to her mezzanine level. She is sitting on her bed, blood all over the covers. She is holding the grey teddy with the love heart. Her face is red and blotchy with tears. I sit on the bed next to her and put my arm around her.

'What's going on, Marilyn?'

She cries and cries. Between sobs she says, 'I'm s-s-scared.'

'Is it the wasps?'

She nods.

'Is it something else, too?'

She nods.

'Can you tell me about it?'

She shakes her head.

'Okay, can you stand up?'

I see that she has cut the tops of her legs. The blood on the bedding makes it look worse than it actually is.

'Why don't you go and have a shower and get cleaned up while I sort out the bed?'

There is a washing machine in their kitchen so I strip the bed and, as I do, the phone slips onto the floor. I pick it up. I press the button and see loads of text and WhatsApp messages. I can't bloody read them because I haven't got my glasses. They're in the other villa. If I can make out the words 'babe' and 'bad girl'.

Marilyn is moving about downstairs. I don't want her to think I'm snooping, when of course that's exactly what I'm doing. But what I've seen is enough to convince me that I need to do some serious detective work.

By the time she comes back up I've stripped the bed, put a wash on and put some fresh sheets on that I discovered in the wardrobe. I'll put the duvet cover back on when it's dry tomorrow.

Lloyd comes in and tells me he's left the children in our room.

'Tell you what, they can bunk up there tonight and I'll sleep here,' I suggest. I settle Marilyn down with a cup of tea in front of the TV and put a film on. Lloyd and I lift up two mattresses from the children's beds and carry them to our villa. We put them on the floor by our bed. One of the boys can sleep on the bed next to their dad. I go back and fetch their bedding. I make sure that they are all secure and safe, say goodnight and head back to the other villa. I stay up with Marilyn until she finally asks to go to bed, way into the small hours of the morning.

Once she's tucked in, I get into Lily's bed and fall into an uneasy sleep.

XV

We're a week into the holiday and I'm no further forward in finding out about Marilyn's phone. I also feel diabolical. I'm ill with a stinking cold. Maybe I picked it up on the plane. Who knows? The others seem to be okay.

But mostly I feel down because I have slept in the large villa with Marilyn every night since she cut her legs. This has become the new arrangement: the others are crammed into the small villa next door but one. I suggested to Marilyn that the two of us move there and let the others have the larger villa, but she refused. She's impossible to please. If I say anything that she doesn't like she begins to scream and shout. Because we are on holiday and the villa walls are thin, I end up letting her have her own way. It seems like the only solution.

Consequently, I have not seen much of the children. They are keeping a wide berth and I don't blame them. I pop into their villa in the mornings, just to see them, but I can't leave Marilyn alone for too long. I'm worried that she will cut herself again. I'm on the lookout constantly. I notice more cuts on her arms.

Lloyd brought back a pack of elastic bands from the supermarket. I've put one on each of Marilyn's wrists to encourage her to flick them instead of cutting herself.

Lloyd takes the children down to the beach each day. I daren't take Marilyn back there, which means I'm stuck here, in our villa complex. I don't quite know why, but the size of the crowds and the hordes of sunbathers seem to send her in a spin. She has become increasingly clingy around me, which, to be honest, I'm struggling with. This is our beloved, much-anticipated family holiday and I am not enjoying it at all.

I just want to go home.

This morning I have to whip round and clean up the small villa. It's got four people living in what is essentially a double room with only a tiny kitchen and a balcony. Then I clear up the big villa. The children still like coming in to watch the widescreen TV, and to shower and bathe in the evenings.

Marilyn has chewed her nails to the quick. They look raw and sore. I try to entice her to the pool to sunbathe. Her fake tan has left streaks of dark orange on ankles and knees. She isn't interested. Her face is pale and blotchy. She is not bothering with her make-up or hair at all. Because I'm so used to seeing her fully made-up, she looks somehow incomplete without it all. Her hair is going greasy without all the attention she usually gives it.

I try tempting her outside with an ice cream. I have also learnt that Marilyn loves anything to do with watermelons.

'They have these lovely watermelon ice creams at the pool bar, Marilyn,' I tell her. 'You'll love them.'

'No thanks.'

After I've cleared up, and tried to dismiss the Cinderella feelings that threaten to wash over me, I decide to sit in the villa garden and sunbathe. I love being outside. Every holiday my natural inclination is to be outside all day long, and all evening, for as long as I can. I feel trapped inside this villa with its heavy, depressing atmosphere. The walls are all too familiar, and seem to be closing in on me after seven days and nights. From the garden I can hear the sounds of fun being had in the pool, even if I can't see it.

But, to my joy, Marilyn agrees to come to the pool. Perhaps the lure of the watermelon ice cream has worked its magic.

I begin to gather my bits and pieces.

'I'm going to have a shower and do my hair first,' she declares.

I sit out in the garden for another two hours.

By lunchtime she is ready, full make-up, white swimsuit and the Adidas shorts. Most people are at the beach so we get the best sun loungers and settle down.

'Would you like to come in for a swim?' I ask, dipping my (still-chipped) toes into the deliciously cool water.

'I can't swim.'

Hallelujah, I think. Finally we're getting to the bottom of what's going on here.

I notice there are a few pool accessories for sale in the snack bar. I buy some arm bands and a ring for Marilyn, blow them up and invite her into the pool's shallow end. She keeps her shorts on in the water, no doubt to cover up the cuts on her legs. I hold her hand and steady her as we step along the mosaic bottom. She is actually smiling again.

'It's fine, Marilyn, you're doing well.'

She beams.

I turn to face her. 'Right, now give me both your hands. That's it.'

I remember how we first taught the boys to swim when they were young. I tell her to relax and to keep holding onto my hands and just let her body and legs float up. She immediately begins to kick in a frenzy. I hold her tight. She is dribbling and spluttering and laughing all at the same time. I begin to walk along the shallowest part of the pool, Marilyn in tow. She is smiling and looking very pleased with herself.

Swimming is part of the National Curriculum for primary schools, so this is another indication that Marilyn hasn't had a continuous education. It makes sense to keep our children safe by teaching them to swim, but beyond the basics at school, it's often left to families. That's if they can afford swimming lessons, and if they choose to prioritise them. So the poor are left to drown, as in so many other areas of life.

It's almost as if Marilyn has never been in a pool before. Children in care seem to miss out on so much more than family.

Being out here with Marilyn means that I feel happier in myself, too. I must admit I have been feeling depressed, but every time I acknowledge that, I think of my Australian friend who is a therapist and convinced, in that practical, no-nonsense Australian way, that depression can *sometimes* be a form of 'sulking for adults'. I hear her words, in her distinctive accent inside my head and I feel ashamed because yes, if I'm completely honest, I am feeling sorry for myself and petulant and sulky as a result.

I get Marilyn to hold on to the side of the pool for the next stage of our impromptu swimming lesson. I put my hand underneath her tummy to hold her up and encourage her to slow down on the kicking. 'Try to relax and enjoy a calmer leg movement.'

She is so happy. Achieving something new is simple dopamine. Thinking about swimming lessons reminds me that I still don't actually know anything about Marilyn's educational history. I know she must have been to school at some stage because the referral said she had been excluded. But how much time has she spent in education? That bit of intel appears not to have made it to the referral.

'What school were you at, Marilyn?'

She can't remember, which is a strange response, but she's preoccupied now with the swimming.

From the safety of holding on to the side, I show her how to move her legs for the breaststroke.

She finds that hilarious. 'Breast stroke?'

I haven't quite got the joke. 'Yes. It's a nice easy stroke for swimming and it keeps your boobs firm and upwards.'

Now I definitely have her attention. I have got my own attention, actually, as I think I may do 100 lengths of the pool every day to drag my boobs away from my knees. I am making myself smile at least, so that's good.

Another friend, Sophie, who is French and a physiotherapist, once told me that with her patients who are sad and have depression, she encourages them to put a pen in their mouth horizontally, in order to force the facial muscles into a smiling expression. As a consequence, they feel happier. Apparently, it also makes you find jokes funnier. While it seems gimmicky, there's science behind it, according to Sophie. When you smile, your brain activates neurotransmitters, little messengers telling the body to release chemicals. A mixture of dopamine, endorphins and serotonin: all associated with lowering anxiety and increasing feelings of happiness. In fact, serotonin is often the chemical that antidepressant medications attempt to regulate. When I'm feeling down in the dumps, I might look like an idiot doing it, but putting a pen across my chops combined with going for a walk is the best thing.

I feel so much better being outside in the sunshine and seeing Marilyn smile. Her smile has been hard to find since coming on holiday. She splashes about with increasing confidence and absolute glee. She wants to show me, every minute, that she is becoming braver. She reminds me of when children are about four or five and want to show you everything. Even if it does get a little dull, we keep smiling and say, 'Well done, clever girl!'

I keep saying this to Marilyn. She thrives on the praise. The way she is reacting gives me the sense that she perhaps didn't get much play and adventure in her early childhood. It's so important. I'm looking at a 13-year-old girl who dresses like a 32-year-old woman and wears make-up like a drag queen. She is so sophisticated in many ways and so childish in others.

When I take away the lens of resentment at a ruined holiday, I see more and more a little girl who just needs love and positive attention. It's heart-breaking and moving and rewarding all at the same time. But I'm still sad that I am not having the holiday I wanted with my family. No matter how magical these moments are with Marilyn – and they are – I am missing my children.

Out of the pool, I order some toasties and drinks. Marilyn sits down on my lounger next to me. Being in close proximity in the swimming pool has generated a kind of intimacy. She wants to tell me something.

'You were asking about school earlier.'

'I was.'

'I was excluded from school. I don't really want to talk about why.'

'Fair enough.'

'But the police had to be involved. And Alan – that's Mum's boyfriend – wasn't pleased. Not because of what I'd done, because he does drugs himself, but because he didn't want the police sniffing around his shops.'

As worldly as she might seem at times, Marilyn goes blithely on, not realising that she's inadvertently told me the reason she was excluded; although given her mention of police involvement, it would have been fairly easy to draw that conclusion.

'So the atmosphere at home, in the palace, wasn't very nice.'

Interesting that home is 'the palace'.

'So then I got a social worker. And Alan liked that even less. The social worker asked if I could stay with a relative. I think Mum would have said no, but she never has a chance against him. Alan said that he'd already been to see my grandparents. I was shipped off like an Amazon parcel. They tried to make me believe in their religion. I received a full-on concentrated conversion plan.'

'Oh, Marilyn.'

'But I wasn't going to do anything that creep told me to.'

The food and drink arrive. Marilyn sits back on her lounger and picks up her phone. I sit on my lounger to eat, offering Marilyn her plate. She is shivering and doing the wobbling bottom lip. Perhaps all this talking has opened up some of the trauma that she's evidently experienced. How awful to have been rejected by her mother like that. It sounds as though she understands that her mother was coerced, though. I try to lighten the mood.

'Well, well, well. Who knew? Marilyn, or should I say Marilyn the Fish, you were a natural in the water.'

She flashes me a look, briefly, as if she wants to agree and talk more, but the shivering has taken over. She takes her plate and has a couple of mouthfuls.

I eat all of mine, with gusto, and then feel fat. Why do I feel fat? A week ago I was proudly declaring that I wasn't worried about my body in a swimsuit. My toenails look awful. I am tired and full of cold which has evolved over the last few days and now presents itself as a sore throat and runny nose.

I sneeze into the towel since I haven't brought out any tissues.

Marilyn pulls her legs up onto the lounger, away from me and my germs. She sits back, looks at her phone and says, 'That's disgusting.'

All our closeness evaporates immediately.

I'm about to argue that it's better than spraying my germs all over everyone, but realise that my words will fall on deaf ears.

I sit back on my lounger and feel drowsy in the sunshine. I drift off, do the nodding dog for a few minutes, then let go.

Marilyn knocks my arm. 'Louise, you're snoring.'

I come to abruptly. All the joy from earlier has seeped away. I now feel fat, full of cold, tired, a failure, and I'm snoring in public. I hate my life. Marilyn asks if she can have an ice cream. I say yes of course, I go to my bag and pull out my purse. I hand over five euros. She looks at me as if I have just passed her a pile of steaming poo.

'I'm not going. You go and get it for me.'

I look at her, incredulous. 'I don't want an ice cream, and the last time I looked, I wasn't your servant. So, if you want an ice cream, Marilyn, you will have to get off that lounger and go and get it!'

'Alright, keep your fucking hair on!'

I can't let that go. 'Marilyn, this is a communal space. Please do not swear and offend other people.'

I notice a German couple in the corner under parasols reading their books. Or at least I assume they are German, since their book titles are in German. Nevertheless, I don't imagine they want to be disturbed on their peaceful poolside afternoon by a teenage strop. After a few minutes of grunting and snarling, Marilyn ties her towel around her waist and struts off huffily to the snack hut.

I watch with some interest as she transforms from an angry lioness into a sugar babe with all the right moves. I see her charm Persephone and her brother instantly. Mainly Persephone's brother, to be fair, who jumps up from his chair to serve her.

She walks back towards me with her watermelon ice cream. I think she is about to say thank you, but instead she does the Ali G hand-thing and says, 'water melown' with a pronounced glottal stop. She laughs and sits down. She is straight back on the phone, which has not stopped pinging all day. I really need to find a way to get at that phone.

For about another 30 minutes or so she is reasonably quiet and well-behaved. Then, all of a sudden, she decides that she is bored.

'Would you like to go back to the villa?' I ask.

I a about to give her the key when she jumps up. She looks down at her legs. 'Why aren't I brown?'

I start to give her the careful-tanning spiel once more, but she cuts me off.

'This is shit. I want to go home. What's the fucking point of coming here if I don't go brown?'

I can feel eyes upon us. I stand up and with the key in my hand. 'Come on. You can go and watch some TV.'

She storms off ahead of me, leaving all her stuff and the unfinished ice cream on her lounger, which is now hosting two wasps. I do not say a word. I open the door of the villa, and the French doors into the garden. The garden wall is the one that runs along the pool. I decide that I can keep an ear out for her from the lounger.

I get her a drink and say, 'There you go. I'm going back to the pool to sunbathe. You know where I am.'

XVI

In the absence of tissues, I take a loo roll from the villa back to the pool and hide it in my bag. My throat hurts and my nose is streaming. I sit on the sun lounger under a parasol feeling utterly fed up. I should keep a diary of what's been happening. There is nothing else that I can do here but record the catalogue of events.

Imagine calling the out of hours team and telling them that they need to pick up Marilyn. I can just envisage how that would go down. I wonder if that has ever happened. But I should let them know. I have a small sketchbook in my bag and a pen and sit sniffing and coughing, writing the record of the holiday from arriving at Gatwick to the present. I must remember to do it every day. What with looking after Marilyn and keeping on top of the housework in the villas, it feels as if I'm working non-stop on this holiday. We worked and saved hard to come here. We were looking forward to it. I've hardly seen the children or Lloyd. It all comes out on the page as I write.

I write about the huge row I had with Lloyd the other evening. It had been building up for days, but without the privacy to vent our frustrations, it stayed bottled up. Until we exploded. He moaned about all the time I was spending with Marilyn and complained that I should be with him more. He went on about how much money we had lost. I let rip in riposte, then sat in the toilet with a towel on my face, screaming.

I hate arguing. I find it so stressful. But I can't even talk properly about how I feel because he, for some stupid reason, made it all about him. I hated him in that moment. I really did. It all seemed so unfair.

Afterwards I went and sat by the pool on a lounger in the dark. Eventually he came out with a glass of wine and apologised. That's how much stress we are under.

We both agreed that this was all down to Freda and her machinations, but if we were in court the prosecution barrister would ask, 'Why didn't you say no?'

How do you argue against that? 'We didn't want to hurt Marilyn's feelings on the day we met her?' It doesn't stand up. It would sound pathetic. It is pathetic. It's all pathetic.

I'm pathetic.

She is a hurt girl who needs attention and nurture, but so do the boys and Lily. Time to 'man up', I think to myself, using an expression I hate – because, as we all know, what that really means is 'woman up'. I make a plan. There is a hotel down the lane that has a dinner menu. It's not as far as the beach restaurants and might be a good opportunity for us all to go out and have dinner. Everyone is enthusiastic, even Marilyn.

We decide to rendezvous at 6.30pm by the steps.

I have a shower, wash my hair and sneeze a lot. I have packed some paracetamol so I take two and soon feel better. Marilyn appears, only a few minutes after the appointed time. She has chosen another clingy T-shirt dress for the occasion.

We all walk to the restaurant in good spirits. Marilyn is joining in and talking, mostly to Lily. As we enter the hotel garden we are welcomed by a short, slim man who is totally charming. The most refreshing character I have seen for a good few days. He welcomes us as 'family'.

'Where would you like to sit?' he asks, offering us the choicest seats with a flourish. We all crowd around a table and order drinks.

Marilyn puts her phone next to her on the table, as does Lily in turn, like cowboys with their pistols in a saloon. Marilyn places her fake Gucci bag on the back of her chair.

'Where are the toilets?'

I spotted them on the way in and point her in the right direction.

She picks up her phone and takes Lily with her to the loo.

I'm curious about the handbag after the trainers revelation on the walk back when we were at home. How long ago that now seems. I lift it up from the chair and peer closely at it. It is perfect. There are no loose threads, no cheap manufacturing. If it's a copy, it's a very good one. I flip up the tag and see two rows of numbers: the bag's own individual code. It is genuine.

Lloyd looks at me with a questioning eyebrow. I put it back and quietly tell him what I've discovered. The boys overhear me.

'Oh, yeah. She's got loads of authentic stuff.'

I look at Lloyd again. If I'm honest, I don't feel that I have completely gotten over our argument from the other night, so I don't look at him with the same kind of connection that we usually have, but I do need him as an ally. We are business partners looking after the children.

'Well, Emily, Marilyn's mum, is into clothes, fashion and vintage. Maybe she's supplying her daughter with the classics,' I say uncertainly, remembering with a frown how she said the bracelet hadn't come from her.

The girls come back then, flicking their hair and moving in a way that is just a little more noticeable than it was before.

I soon spot the motivation for their change in demeanour. There is a family on the other side of the garden. Two adults and two sons, older than the girls, and definitely older than Jackson and Vincent.

I assume the familiar 'watching like a hawk' alertness.

We all enjoy a lovely dinner. The nicest meal of the holiday. The food is great. There is laughter and minimal flirting across the tables. The 'hello, family' man is lovely, in spite of Marilyn and Lily insisting to him that, 'We're not family.' It's the only blot on the evening and, if I'm honest, it hurts more than a little, especially coming from Lily who has been with us for years now She feels like family to us. Still, at least things are calm. A reasonably sane and pleasant evening, all told.

Eventually we leave the restaurant and walk back up the lane to the villas. The boys are jumping on and off walls, while the girls seem to have become 'besties'. I walk alongside Lloyd and he holds my hand. That eases my resentment towards him a little. I'm still thawing since the argument, but it helps. The kids all pile in the big villa and we head over to the small one for some wine and to sit on the balcony for a while.

This is a pattern that we have established. It seems to work better for part of the evening. Then I go to the big villa later on to sleep in order to keep an eye on Marilyn. But for an hour at least, I can relax.

We're having a peaceful time. We're even laughing. It is so needed. Lloyd is telling me about Jackson burying Vincent at the beach and I giggle as he shows me a picture of Vincent grinning, up to his neck in sand. Then we hear a sudden loud knock at the door. I immediately jump up and open the door to discover Persephone outside.

'Your child, the girl, is out of control.'

I call Lloyd, who follows me and Persephone to the

swimming pool. Marilyn has pushed the loungers into the pool. She is skipping around its perimeter, shouting, 'I hate you all.'

Lily sits in the corner huddled up, crying. The boys are watching over their villa's garden wall.

'Marilyn, you need to stop and come with me.'

Lloyd gets in the pool fully clothed and begins retrieving the loungers. His mouth is set in a grim line. He is livid, and doing his best to remain calm.

I lead Marilyn into the villa. Her phone is on the table, pinging away, as ever. I go to pick it up to give to her. She freaks out and starts shouting and screaming. 'Put that fucking thing down!'

Lloyd, by now, has reached the door. He's dripping wet, but pulls Jackson, Vincent and Lily away to take them to the other villa.

I can hear Persephone talking to other guests, who are complaining.

I don't blame them. This is awful.

I close the door, both to shut out the complaints and to prevent Marilyn from disturbing anyone further. No such luck. Marilyn starts kicking the furniture. She pulls the curtains off the French windows, still screaming.

She is like a wild thing. I genuinely don't know what to do. I feel scared, for myself and for her. She heads towards the kitchen drawer and reaches for a knife. I move so fast I don't have time to think. I push her out of the way and slam the drawer shut. I thought I had removed everything sharp days ago, but I think the cleaners must have replaced the missing cutlery.

I stand in front of her and, in the most authoritative tone I can muster, command her. 'Stop this, Marilyn. Go and sit down.'

She is not herself. It is as if she is under a spell. Suddenly she starts to cry. I hold her hand and walk her to the sofa. We sit down amid the carnage created in the last few minutes. I can see a substantial bill coming.

I don't say a word, just sit with her, holding her hand. I don't know what to say. I don't have words. That bloody phone is still pinging. I want to launch it over the villa wall and into the pool.

XVII

Marilyn must have made her way to her bed at some point because when I wake up I am still sitting upright on the sofa, alone, sunlight streaming through the now curtainless windows. I feel more tired than ever, and as soon as I recall the events of last night I feel a sinking feeling within, and I'm once more demoralised.

Lloyd appears in the kitchen with a coffee. 'How are you doing?'

I shrug.

'I've spoken to Persephone this morning. She told me she's received complaints from other guests and, if Marilyn does one more thing that affects their stay, we'll all be asked to move.' His voice is cheery and matter of fact, but my heart sinks.

I go up to the mezzanine level to check on Marilyn. She is fast asleep, holding the great fluffy love heart teddy and sucking her thumb. Her phone is by her head. I walk over and see loads of message notifications. It is incessant.

'How are the children?' I ask Lloyd.

He laughs. 'They're still sleeping, of course. But last night they could not stop talking about Marilyn pushing all the loungers into the pool. I think that one will go down in family folklore.'

I go and sit outside so Marilyn can't hear us. I close the door behind me. Lloyd eyes up the fallen curtain and the runner.

'That's not too bad. I can fix it.'

'Good, or we'll be homeless. Homeless in Skiathos.'

'Like Sleepless in Seattle only not as romantic.'

'Not romantic at all. And I'm also Sleepless in Skiathos.'

I smile. Definitely thawing. We pause and sip our coffee in companionable peace for a few moments.

'I keep thinking about that bloody phone, you know. I want to know who she is communicating with. She won't tell me.'

Lloyd, ever pragmatic, says, 'We only have four days to go. Is it worth the fight? We need to keep her calm and get to the end, get out of here and get home.'

I sigh and agree. This has become a test of endurance as much as anything else.

He asks, 'How about I book a boat?'

It's one of the things we always do on holiday and it might be something that Marilyn would enjoy. I smile. 'Yes, I would love that.'

He leaves to go to the beach with the children and I drag

out time with 'Hello Family' at the hotel next door. I pay to use their pool rather than the one that we have free access to because Marilyn hasn't blotted her copybook there yet. She loves the pool, mostly because the boys from the other night are there. She is in full posing flirty mode.

I decide to let her get on with it. I'm on the lounger, watching, and have already made eye contact with the boys' mum and smiled. What could possibly go wrong under two pairs of watchful eyes?

Time passes. I'm not sure quite how to feel. I know they call it 'compassion fatigue' or 'blocked care', this shift when you suddenly can't find it in you to keep trying to support your child or young person. It happens a lot and to good people.

It's happening to me, now.

The trouble is that when it happens we do not feel comfortable talking about it. It can be seen as failure. We can be on our knees and yet be too afraid to ask for help, because then we are 'not coping'. We are seen as weak if we can't cope. Also, many carers become financially dependent on their foster income because often local authorities or agencies insist one them has to be at home, effectively meaning the loss of one income. Then it can become really messy as the foster carers are in crisis but daren't say anything in case they lose their income. It's a terribly unfair situation. Foster carers cannot look after traumatised children when they are stressed, it's as simple as that. The reality is that most of us *are* stressed and daren't ask for help, mainly because there isn't any help. They have to book meetings and have more meetings with professionals that you or the children have never met to decide your fate. It's actually perverse. But the longer I think about it the crosser I get, and I'm on holiday now, when I really shouldn't be thinking about these things.

I am definitely feeling a little bit of this shift today. I'm still smarting after hearing Lily say 'they're not my family' to Hello Family man. I suspect that she did not mean it the way it sounded, but at the time, it was a blow.

By lunchtime I'm chatting to the boys' mum, Astrid, who is a teacher from Denmark. I unburden myself and tell her what's been going on. She is lovely and kind and talks about similar social issues in Denmark, and how their education and children's services work. They sound, at least from her description, like they work much better than ours. Still, in the current climate, that's quite a low bar.

Marilyn is a little disgruntled that we are chatting, but at least I've given the boys' mum the heads-up, so I am sure she will make sure that nothing daft happens.

God, the last thing we need is a pregnant Marilyn!

XVIII

It's the boat trip today.

I'm actually very excited. We like to stop off on an island and have some lunch. The children like to do a bit of snorkelling. I have hardly had any time with the boys or Lily so far, so I'm really looking forward to spending time with them. This has been a difficult trip in so many ways. I can't get away from the fact that we have paid an enormous amount of money, that we worked hard for, to basically have a crap time.

It's awful.

I'm finding it an increasing struggle to keep up with Marilyn's demands. It's harder and harder to be supportive of her. This is the compassion fatigue setting in, certainly, but I also think she is 'playing us' to a certain degree. There are patterns to her behaviour that seem calculated. For example, she knows that there are other people at the villa complex, and that we are anxious not to 'make a scene'.

She is quick to point out that we can't shout at her. And yes, I know that we are not meant to; we are meant to de-escalate by talking quietly and calmly, but in the heat of the moment I would challenge anyone who is as tired as me, and as demoralised as me, not to raise their voice in a crisis. My 'headmistress voice' did the trick with the knife in the kitchen, and its use was instinctive. I didn't have time to think about the rights and wrongs of shouting.

When Barbara, my adoptive mother, became ill and needed round-the-clock residential care, I saw her choose her behaviour. She would behave appallingly in public – then, when I took her home, feeling drained and humiliated, she would say, 'I pushed you too far, I'm sorry.'

There is something disturbingly familiar about Marilyn's behaviour that reminds me of Barbara. She seems to turn it on and turn it off. If we were in our normal home environment, I would leave her to it. I would take myself and others away to remove her audience so that she could not perform. But that is impossible here in a villa complex with other guests in ringside seats.

I think she is looking for attention, seeking it out. Constructing these mortifying situations, like with the topless German women, or the sun loungers in the pool. And that bloody phone! What is it with the phone? I keep having dark thoughts about that phone. Maybe when we're on the boat it could 'accidentally' fall overboard.

No, Louise, that's a terrible notion. I'm ashamed to even think it. But I do think it. At least on the boat there will be no audience. Only us. It should be possible to have a nice day.

I double check the villas to make sure everything is turned off and shipshape. Lloyd and I have checked and double-checked that the crew have everything. I am excited and as we are so close to the end of the holiday from hell, I feel a sense of abandon. I walk alongside Jackson and Vincent, who are buzzing with excitement. They love going on boat trips. We call into the supermarket and get cheese and ham rolls, crisps, biscuits, cakes and plenty of drinks.

Ahoy there!

We walk through the crowd of sunbathers at the beach. I no longer care if Marilyn is struggling with the concept of women of all shapes and sizes tanning their bodies. Lloyd walks into the boat hut and sorts out the paperwork. Marilyn is chewing her fingernails and sucking her thumb.

A lovely lady comes out of the hut and introduces herself. She is the wife of the boatman. I instantly like her: she is fun and cheery, but also no-nonsense and strong. She clocks Marilyn's state straight away.

'Are you feeling scared?'

An accurate observation, but I'm not sure it's a good idea to draw attention to it, given my suspicions about Marilyn and her attention-seeking.

The nice lady ('Call me Athena, like the goddess') goes through the health and safety requirements and shows us a laminated map of the islands, pointing out the best spots to head for.

Marilyn shifts from foot to foot. I get a feeling that she is working herself up. Athena-like-the-goddess does her best to encourage Marilyn to the boat. Marilyn walks alongside her, behind the rest of us. I put our bags in the boat and the boys are first aboard, followed by Lloyd and Lily. I call Marilyn. She hangs back on the beach, shivering and crying.

'I can't do it. I can't do it. I can't do it. I'm scared.'

We all try to entice her on board.

After a few minutes of cajoling, Jackson exclaims, 'For fuck's sake.'

I haven't really heard this language from Jackson before and it's not even whispered under his breath. Nevertheless, he is echoing my own thoughts. And I shouldn't be surprised: he is well-ensconced at secondary school where they become fluent in Year 7.

Marilyn starts to scream and walk around in circles and, once again, the crowd is watching. She *is* good at playing to an audience.

I say, 'Right. That's that, then.'

I get my bag with my keys and purse and jump back on the beach. There's no other option. We can't let the other kids down, and I won't take the boat out by myself. This is Captain Lloyd's gig.

Captain Lloyd looks at me with a kind of despairing compassion. This was my last chance to feel like I was on holiday. I feel like crying. But just as the tears threaten to spring forth, I can hear my bloody Australian friend's voice echoing in my head: 'Depression can be sulking for adults.'

Athena-like-the-goddess walks up to me and says, 'It's okay. She can stay here with me. You go with your husband and the other children.'

Oh, I am so tempted. Sorely, sorely tempted. But I can't do that. I know exactly how it would sound if Marilyn ever said anything to a social worker.

'Louise and Lloyd left me with complete strangers for the day, while they went off and had fun on a boat trip.'

It can't play out like that. I thank her profusely and say that Marilyn is our foster child.

'I can't leave her. We will go back to the villa. Don't worry about us.'

The boat lady is so kind and bloody understanding and caring that I feel like crying again. I look at Marilyn and take a deep breath. She is hugging herself with her phone pressed against her arm.

I wave goodbye to my family.

'Have a lovely day. Take some photos for me!'

There are tears in my eyes and there is nothing I can do about it.

XIX

'Come on, Marilyn. Let's go and have a coffee.'

We sit in one of the nearest beach restaurants for a while. I watch the world go by. The other holidaymakers with smiles on their faces, relaxed and enjoying themselves.

To cheer myself up I decide to have an early lunch.

'What would you like?' I ask Marilyn.

She sits with her head down and pulls a red baseball cap out from her bag. She puts it on, pulls it down and shuts off. Charming.

I ask again. 'Marilyn, would you like a drink? Or perhaps an ice cream?'

She nods.

The waiter comes over. I order myself a pitta bread feast with hummus, olives, tzatziki, baba ganoush, the works.

When it arrives, Marilyn looks at the olives and turns her nose up in disdain. 'They're disgusting.'

I reply with the same words I have said to so many foster children when they are near food that is not a pot noodle or chicken nuggets. 'I might think your food choices are disgusting, but I would never be so rude to say so. Please do not comment on other people's food, especially when you have never even tried it.'

With that, my latte arrives, along with a glass of water for Marilyn, who pipes up, 'Can I have what you're having, please?'

I ask the waiter for another plate of Greek gorgeousness. I smile at Marilyn. 'Sometimes it's good to try something new. You never know, you may enjoy it.' I stop short of adding 'variety is the spice of life, after all,' before I turn into a parody of myself.

In response, Marilyn turns her baseball cap to a jaunty Norman Wisdom angle. She enjoys her plate of food, although the olives would have been a step too far, so I eat them on her behalf. We sit and look out to sea for a while. She points at a boat on the horizon and says, 'Is that them?'

I shrug. Who knows from this distance?

As we get up from our table I notice Marilyn looking intently at something. She seems very distracted. I turn around to see what's bothering her.

There is an English couple, probably in their 60s, at a nearby table, minding their own business. She is staring at them in a way that would be uncomfortable for anyone to experience. It's becoming a little obvious. I smile apologetically at the couple who are looking at the menu, trying to pretend they aren't under scrutiny.

'Good afternoon!' I call out. I'm so used to sweeping up the debris that Marilyn leaves in her wake it feels like second nature to be apologising to total strangers. 'We'll just be on our way. Excuse us.'

Marilyn is still staring.

'Come on, Marilyn. Let's go.'

When we get outside, I ask, 'Are you okay? What was all that about? What happened back there?'

'He – she breaks off with a puzzled frown. 'He upset me.'

'What do you mean he upset you? He didn't do anything that I could see.'

'He looks like my grandad.'

Having met her grandfather for all of two minutes on the doorstep, I think she's right.

'Yes, I can see the likeness, now that you mention it. But it wasn't him.' I'm sure of that because I can't imagine that fun-sucker going on a summer holiday to Skiathos.

She pulls down her baseball cap and says, 'He's a paedophile.'

'Your grandad is?'

She nods and shudders, making a strange whinnying sound, like a horse.

There was no mention of abuse on her referral form, so perhaps she hasn't told anybody before. That's quite a disclosure. I don't know whether to leave it there, or get my metaphorical tweezers out and prise more from her. I opt for the latter.

'Marilyn, did he hurt you?'

She doesn't hesitate. 'Yeah. He did.'

I say, 'I'm sorry, Marilyn. I really am. That's a horrible thing to have to live with.'

She says, 'He's disgusting. I hate him.'

'Have you told anyone else?' I say.

She shrugs. Then she leans forward conspiratorially. 'Mum knows.'

My heart is aching. All is forgiven. No wonder she thought he was a creep. I reach out, take her hand and hold it as we walk back to the villa. My mind is working overtime. The way she said 'Mum knows' made me shiver. Did she mean that she has told Emily – or that Emily knows because she's experienced it too?

I can't ask her. But I will need to report it as soon as we get back.

Marilyn puts her thumb in her mouth as we walk, her phone in her bag for once. I want to know who keeps messaging her, but one small step at a time.

That was huge.

XX

Back at the villas, Persephone is talking to her mother and the cleaners. We walk past and I say, 'Hello,' cheerfully but keep walking. Head down, ploughing on. I don't want any trouble. I want to stay close to Marilyn, who might want to say more about what happened to her. She might not, but either way I am now signed up to support Marilyn in every way I can, without crying on her behalf. I'm not sure how helpful that would be.

We arrive at our villas. I arrange to call for her on the way to the pool. I gather my notebook and pen because I have a lot to add to my records and reflections about the trip. We find two loungers and drag them across to a sunny spot. I'm happy to be here and, to be honest, if anyone now so much as whispers about Marilyn, I will have their guts for garters.

She pushes her lounger close to mine and sunbathes for a while, after I have smothered her in factor 50.

She looks at me, concerned. 'I'm still not going brown.'

I say, 'Darling, you are an English rose. Beautiful. But it means the best you can hope for is a pretty pink, then gold.'

She frowns.

'You've left it a bit late to work on your tan. For these last two days, I'd just suggest making the most of it. We have the rest of the summer ahead. You can get a nice base here and then top up back in England.'

I'm talking to myself as much as Marilyn. I'm not tanned at all, not really, and my toenails *still* look awful, even worse than when we arrived. I never got around to buying that varnish and sorting them out. But I have begun to understand Marilyn and feel protective of her, as I did that first time we went to the beach back in England. As I watch the men around the pool, I wonder which ones have abused children and women in some way. That's an awful way to think, but I can't help it after Marilyn's disclosure. It's the lens I am wearing today.

We hang around the pool all afternoon with no major incidents. I think the reality of going home tomorrow sits comfortably with both of us. Every now and then I say something like, 'You must pack *tonight*. Don't leave it until the morning.' Or, 'Make sure you leave out restaurant clothes and travel clothes.'

When it gets to 4pm and there is still no sign of Lloyd and the children, I suppress my fear for their safety and I tell myself that they are in a well-monitored, heavily-protected tourist zone and Lloyd's parents were both in the Navy. Not that that means much at all; my adopted dad was a heating engineer but I haven't a clue how to fix the boiler.

'Time's marching on,' I say after a few more minutes' fretting. 'I'm going to go and start packing the others' suitcases so that we have a bit of a head start.'

Marilyn gets up and follows me to the big villa. 'Can I help you?'

Wow. That's a turnaround. But I don't register any surprise. I just ask her to gather everything up 'and put it in a rough pile near the suitcase'.

She does this for a while, and then sits on the sofa with her phone.

'Are you playing a game?' I ask.

She shakes her head, eyes fixed firmly on the screen. I have my reading glasses in my bag. I put them on and busy myself in the villa gathering clothes and shoes. I hover behind her and pretend to be tidying. She has no interest in me or what I am doing which, at this precise moment, is trying desperately to read her messages. I catch, *Babe lots to do when you get back xx.*

Who *is* this?

Eventually the others return, having not been lost at sea at all, and instead having had the most fantastic day island-hopping. They are beautifully tanned, sun-kissed from hours on the ocean waves, and happy. They all look so healthy and relaxed, while I am conscious that I look (and feel) like an old hag. But I have a new sense of relief because, this time tomorrow, we will be near England. Everything will be back to normal and I will have some support from social services.

I tell them all how wonderful they look and ask questions about their adventure. Jackson has half a rancid fish in his bucket.

'Uggh! Put it outside the villa. That can't stay in here!'

I hear all about how fantastic their day has been, each keen to tell me about 'the best bit'.

Lily is yawning, and they are all very hungry. I open a packet of crisps and pour them into a bowl to keep them going whilst they get changed. I go and get changed myself. I shower and wash my hair, blow-drying it with the intention of creating a J-Lo style demi-wave but it doesn't go well and I end up with more of a 'rock chick' look. This is a euphemism for 'messy'. Oh well. I start off with the best intentions and then always lose interest in styling it by the time I get to the back.

By the time we are all ready we look family-fabulous, even if we don't all quite scrub up to the same extent, I shall say for tonight that we do!

Since it's the last night, we decide to pay another visit to 'Hello Family' man's restaurant, which is not only much closer than those on the beach, but has almost become a familiar part of the trip. It's curious how even when we are abroad, away from everything we know, we still end up creating comfortable routines. We all sit down and watch the area fill up.

There is a Greek dancing troupe in the house tonight. I love it. A perfect entertainment for the end of the holiday. We eat and drink, and drink and eat. Lloyd keeps buying me cocktails. I get the children to go up to the bar and order ice creams. They love the grown-upness of that. Sitting on bar stools - they'd never be allowed to do that in a bar at home - they chat to Mr Hello Family and his wife. He has a money box on the bar, in the shape of a red Ferrari.

Vincent asks him what it's for.

'Ah well, you see, I put all my tips in there so that one day I will have enough to buy a Ferrari and drive it to England!'

The children come running back and ask for tip money. It's the last night and I have some cash. I pull out a crisp 20 euro note. Vincent grabs it from my hand and darts back to the bar where I watch him carefully fold it so it fits inside the gap. It might just about buy a flange nut for a Ferrari, but hey.

The garden is full of families and locals. I get a little drunk, I have to confess. After the Greek dancing and some celebratory plate-smashing as a crowd-pleaser for the tourists, ABBA is put on very loudly. I am pulled onto the dance floor by an imaginary force. I am up and dancing, arms everywhere, laughing and clapping my hands. The nice Danish lady, whose name I have forgotten – Astrid, was it? – joins me. She is dancing with abandon and laughing too. Suddenly most of the women are up together, all singing at the top of our voices to *Dancing Queen*. I catch sight of the boys, who look mortified. Lloyd is taking pictures with his phone. He'd better not post them on social media or I'll divorce him. We sing and dance as if all the mums need to kick back. It's such fun. This is what holidays are meant to be.

I glance over and see Lily and Marilyn are now sitting on a low wall near the grass. They are looking at me and whispering. No doubt bitching about me, glad that they are not actually in our family.

I don't care. I've had a totally shit two weeks and tonight they can all bog off and, if Freda was here judging me, I would tell her to bog off too, the sanctimonious old bag.

Yes, I'm a *bit* tipsy.

Lloyd has stopped the photo reportage for a moment and is checking on all the children, seeing if they want more drinks. Meanwhile, ABBA has given way to Fleetwood Mac. We're most definitely in the 'mum's music' section of the evening's entertainment. What fun the Danish mum and I are having, a complete laugh. We giggle when we notice her sons look as mortified as mine. Eventually I sit down and take a sip of another cocktail. This time it's a Black Russian. Delicious. I sit and watch all the people, not thinking about anything in particular, when Marilyn appears. She looms next to me.

'Hello sweetheart, are you okay?' I ask.

She leans forward and says, 'Can I sit on your lap?'

I move my arm out of the way. 'Help yourself.'

Marilyn sits on my lap and snuggles in like a toddler. I find myself rocking her and brushing her hair from her face. I have drunken tears in my eyes as I start singing a Rhiannon song to her. Lily comes over to join us. She sits at my feet holding my leg. I look up at one point and see the nice Danish lady. She blows me a kiss and smiles. I feel full to the brim with love. We stay like this for half an hour or more. Who knows? I've lost all concept of time.

XXI

Back at the villa, the children seem to be getting on well. After the earlier bonding session the girls are now besties and the boys are after sweets. They play and hang out in their villa, most of the packing done. There is an air of calm. Lloyd and I sit on our balcony. We're getting on much better. I no longer want to divorce him because I've remembered that I don't actually hate him.

I'm a little ashamed of my feelings earlier on the holiday, but it's where we can all go when tired and stressed and overburdened. He's alright, my husband, when he's not offloading onto me. We have been tested these past few weeks: emotionally, financially and physically. Why? I have to ask myself. We didn't need any of this but, optimist that I am, I will, when rested, see some good.

I will, I hope, be able to help Marilyn. I have no idea if Emily would support her daughter by reporting the grandfather for abuse. So much goes unreported, which is one reason why these vile people get away with it. Mind you, as far as I know from reading and watching the news and talking to people, institutions like local authorities, churches, boarding schools and so on are very good at closing rank and destroying evidence. But I don't know any more than Marilyn's simple statement of disclosure at this stage.

Lloyd brings me some iced water, obviously recognising that I am still a little drunk. If a social worker were to walk through that door right now and say, 'Louise, have you been drinking?' I would say, 'Yeah, I have. What of it? Want one?'

As if on cue, there is a knock at the door. So far this holiday that has only meant bad news. Lloyd and I exchange looks. We share the automatic feeling of alarm.

I get up first. Thanks, Lloyd. Perhaps he's still on report!

I open the door to discover Marilyn with a washing-up bowl. On her arm is a carrier bag full of stuff. She comes in and walks to the balcony. She puts the bowl on the table. The water is warm and bubbly and sprinkled with flower petals; she must have picked them from the shrubs around the pool. Lloyd and I now share a look of surprise, both of us instantly charmed by Marilyn's sweet offering, whatever is going on here.

'What's all this?'

She puts down her carrier bag and pulls out a folded piece of paper. She places it in my hands. On the outside it says 'Lloyd and Louise' and our names are surrounded by biro-inked drawings of love hearts, flowers and butterflies. I take the paper and open it out.

Dear Louise and Lloyd,

I am sorry for the way I have behaved and for ruining your holiday. I'm ashamed of myself and know that you did a lot for me. Sometimes I don't know why I do these things. It is like having a voice in my head that's telling me to upset people, things. You have been so nice to me and that's lovely. I wish I knew why I did it. I understand if you want me to go.
I love you and I am sorry.
Marilyn

I hand the letter to Lloyd, speechles. Tears are spilling down my face. In a second, tears begin to fall down his face too.

I take Marilyn's hand. 'Thank you. You have no idea how much that means to me. To us.'

She smiles. Her face is the young Marilyn face, the child trapped inside a body that can look so much older than she is.

'Marilyn, I don't know exactly what has happened to you, but after what you told me at the restaurant, I have an inkling. When you are ready we will do whatever we can to help you. In the meantime all we can do is look after you and keep you safe.'

I look at her face and something flashes through it. Fear? I get the distinct feeling that there is more to this than meets the eye. But, as we all know, children need to feel safe before they share. And when they share, precisely because they feel safe, we will see more challenging behaviour. To be able to be of any use to Marilyn and look after the others, I will need to rest and recharge my batteries. Ironically, leaving our holiday behind will enable me to at least sleep and feel calmer because I will be at home and have some sense of control. Oh, this life.

Marilyn wants us to enjoy her relaxing spa and we are very appreciative. 'Louise, would you like a pedicure?'

'Would I ever. Daft question.'

My feet go in the bowl. Lloyd pours me more water then gets the wine. She puts her music on her phone and leaves it on the table. While she is busy removing the traces of my chipped nail polish, I try to look at her phone. I'm sure it's the same phone model, but I'm also certain that it's a different actual phone. I remember when we were in the car at home I saw her fiddling with the corner of the screen cover. It had creases and stuck up a bit at the edge. I have seen her use that phone here too. This one seems to be in far better condition.

'Marilyn, have you bought a new screen protector for your phone?'

She looks at me and shakes her head. 'No,' and carries on.

She asks Lloyd to get a towel, spreads it across her legs and starts work on my feet. She is very good, her gentle, steady hand massaging my heels and the balls of my feet. I have to say this feels the best pedicure I have ever had.

She pulls two bottles of nail polish out of her bag and holds up one in each hand.

'Pale gold-green or electric blue?'

I remember having a similar green on my toenails while I was in Malaysia on a business trip years ago. I was in a lift with three American pilots. They looked down at my newly applied green polish that I was proudly displaying through my red sandals. One of them said, 'Ma'am, your toes seem to have gone mouldy.'

I felt humiliated.

I opt for the electric blue. These days I never wear anything other than orange or red, but electric blue will do. Any port in a storm. She does a wonderful job. I am seeing a side to Marilyn that is beautiful, kind and caring, and very good at all this stuff.

'Do you think you might want to do beauty when you're older?'

She is surprised by my question. 'What, me?'

'Yes, you. You are naturally good at it. You have great style and always look great.'

That's not entirely true: I've seen fake tan more convincingly applied, and there was that day she looked like Widow Twankey, but I'm not going to ruin this beautiful moment by alluding to either of those things.

The others come in and make themselves at home. The boys start rooting through the kitchenette cupboards and are successful in their foraging: one packet of Chittos and four packets of Haribo that I bought days ago and forgot about.

Finally I see happy, contented children and it's 10pm on the last evening.

Better late than never.

XXII

In the morning, the good mood carries over. Everyone wakes up on time. There is no fighting, moaning or vandalism. I have pretty toes. Today is a good day. I have never said this before when leaving a holiday in Greece, but I can't wait to get home.

We have a big breakfast at the hotel next door and see Mr Hello Family for the last time. There isn't much about this holiday that I shall miss, but he is always so welcoming and good at what he does. I hope he made a fortune from his tips. Maybe enough to buy a Ferrari steering wheel if everyone who was having a good time last night contributed to the pot.

The children are chatty and looking forward to the adventure of travelling home, even though Jackson, Vincent and Lily are sad that the holiday is over. Marilyn looks good. She must have slept well. Her skin looks fresh. She is back doing the Ali G hand thing, but today it is funny. Her phone is pinging away already. It must be 8am in England, given the time difference. That's early for youngies in the summer holidays.

I watch her as she looks at the phone. I look at her face, and the way it changes in response to what she reads. I see a frown appear, and she starts chewing her nails. I also notice the curled up edge of the screen protector. It is definitely a different phone. I am utterly convinced of that. I say nothing. I will add these details to my diary for the two-week holiday.

Instead of investigating further, I say to her, 'Marilyn, how about another fruit juice?'

She smiles. 'Yeah, please.'

After breakfast we walk back up the lane to the villas. We walk past the swimming pool and I acknowledge the various guests who I am sure have complained about us, and who can blame them? No one wants trouble when they've paid good money to have a break.

Lloyd and I check all the suitcases and do a sweep around the big villa. We then get our cases and walk them to the reception area and hand in the keys. Persephone smiles, probably glad to see the back of us. She looks hard at Marilyn, and I have a sudden fear. *Oh God, she's going to say something.*

She does say something, but first she approaches Marilyn and gives her a hug. Then she holds both shoulders and says, 'Marilyn you are a beautiful girl. Be brave and do well.'

Wow. I was not expecting that!

We say more goodbyes and I feel lighter knowing that

we are not really a family from *Shameless*, even though we might have done a very good impression of one at repeated points of this holiday. We stand where the taxi will come. Eventually it does. It's a different driver this time. Who is very grumpy. We pile our cases into the boot and on laps. We squeeze in. The driver is very rude. Persephone appears with her mother and just as the driver looks like he is getting back in they walk him to the side. I hear Persephone tear him off a strip in Greek. She is not impressed. She needs good reviews on her website and leaving her villas is the last memory her visitors will have. Her mother has a powerful gravelly voice; she says something too. The two women stand with their arms folded as the driver gets into the taxi.

He is suddenly very polite.

We get to the airport and the driver smiles as he passes us the suitcases. We say goodbye. Lloyd and I look at each other.

Marilyn says, 'He got *roasted*, man' and flicks the Ali G hands. The boys and Lily think it is hilarious. I can't help but join in. The Greek men are not quite as Alpha-male as they like to think.

We hang around the market area buying more food. Even though we've only just had breakfast they all seem to be hungry again. I notice Marilyn moving towards me ready to cling on to me once more. This time I stand near her but do not allow her to attach herself to me. I need her to feel safe but she must learn to stand on her own two feet when she is feeling anxious.

As we head towards the plane I feel her press against my arm. I hold her hand and squeeze it.

'It will be fine, Marilyn. We'll be home soon.' As we board the plane, I realise that the crew know who we are, and are ready to intervene with Marilyn should that be required. That is extremely efficient of the airline, I must say. I'm impressed. We are seated right at the front. This time we organise ourselves so that we have Marilyn in the middle, between Lloyd and me. I'm by the window; he's on the aisle. The pilot appears, looking quite authoritarian.

Marilyn looks up when he leans forward to address her directly.

'Marilyn. I'm pleased to meet you.' He explains that we will take off and then hop to a nearby airport called Thessaloniki to refuel. 'That's because the runway here at Skiathos is short and, if we had a full tank of fuel, the plane would be too heavy to take off.' He goes on to reassure Marilyn that there is nothing to be frightened of and explains all the sounds and movements and how the wind affects the movement of the plane.

Never mind Marilyn, Lloyd is thrilled to bits. If we hadn't already been in aeroplane mode on the phones, I think he would have asked for a selfie with the pilot and put it on Facebook.

The pilot's pre-emptive strike works. This time when we take off she does not scream. She squeezes my hand until it hurts but there are no histrionics. Hooray!

When we are up in the air after refuelling and people are milling about, Marilyn feels brave enough to go to the loo. As she gets up and turns to make the short walk to the toilets, Lloyd hits me on the arm. What is it with people hurting my arms on aeroplanes? On the back of Marilyn's dress is a large blood stain. It shows up prominently against the pale grey of her dress. My heart sinks. I leap up to try and do something. One of the air hostesses has already seen it. I move towards Marilyn and whisper, 'Your period has leaked onto your dress.' My supply of sanitary products is in my suitcase so I don't have anything to offer her. The air hostess has some towels in her handbag. Lloyd brings us Lily's hoodie. She has very kindly taken it off to offer Marilyn as a wrap-around to cover the blooded area. It is a swift operation and although it isn't a nice moment, it's lovely to see the team spring into action. Marilyn is spared from the devastation of humiliation. I don't think anyone else saw, and if they did, well, that's what happens when you are a woman.

Nearly home.

XXIII

The long drive back from Gatwick is terrifying. Lloyd and I are both tired, me especially. We take it in turns and I can feel my eyelids getting heavy. I open the windows to let some fresh air into the car but hear nothing but moaning from the children.

Once back they all go straight to bed. I, however, have a sudden urge of manic energy and know that sleep will be impossible. This is definitely a stress response. Rather than put myself through restless, fruitless tossing and turning, I sit downstairs in the kitchen with a hot drink. The house feels weird at this time of night. An unusual calm has fallen across it. I decide to make a start on the mountains of washing. I empty the suitcases and create piles of darks, lights and whites. In the process, I notice how many of Marilyn's clothes have blood dots on them. Some items are stuck together with dried blood. That's probably why she wanted to wear shorts over her swimsuit, to cover up the cuts at the tops of her thighs.

I see the furry grey teddy with the big love heart. She hasn't taken it to bed with her. I shove that in the wash too. I root through to the bottom and find a square envelope. It's a greetings card. On the front is Marilyn's name and the address is that of her last placement. I pull out the card. It has a saccharine picture of teddies holding hands surrounded by love hearts. Perhaps I shouldn't, but I can't help myself. I open it.

In clumsy lettering, all uppercase and randomly spaced, I read, 'Babe I love you, you're the most beautiful girl in the world.'

My interest is well and truly piqued. So, who is this? I must tread carefully. She is a young girl, only just a teenager. What is going on here? She is obviously emotionally invested in this person but has never mentioned them. It's clearly a romantic relationship, or at least it is in Marilyn's eyes. Something about it feels very wrong to me. The trouble with children who have not had all their emotional and physical needs met is that they are vulnerable to exploitation. And actually, simply having their needs 'met' is not enough: children need people to be aspirational for them, to help them push themselves into better lives.

I don't like this one bit. Something is wrong here and it's time to do some more detective work. It's also time for bed. I have managed three loads of washing and hung as much out on the line in the dark as I can, as well as loading the clothes horse in the conservatory. I've broken the back of it, but there are still a few more loads to be done. Those beach towels are a couple of loads on their own. Suddenly I feel very tired. Just then, the cats come in. I'll go to bed soon. I need to say a proper hello to my fluffy friends. I've missed them this last couple of weeks.

I wake up at 10am, which is unheard of. I'm not quite sure where I am. I look at Lloyd, then around the room and sigh. 'Thank God, we're home.' I turn over and go back to sleep until 11am, finally woken by Jackson who is standing in the doorway asking for food. I did have the brain power last night to get some milk out of the freezer so basically, if they are hungry, they can eat cereal until we've been to the shops, which is roughly what I tell Jackson.

He grunts and heads off down the stairs. I drag myself out of bed, smiling. It doesn't matter if Marilyn's behaviour is off, or challenging, because I'm home and I'm safe and there is a kettle with a tin of proper-tasting teabags. So, bring it on! Tea for me, but not for my cosmopolitan spouse.

'Coffee, Lloyd?'

'Mmmm. Yes.'

I hold myself back from saying, 'Off you go then and make it' and with my best 1950s advertising campaign smile, but stopping short of tying a ribbon in my hair, I whisk myself downstairs to look after my man.

In the kitchen two meowing cats are demanding breakfast. I have no doubt they have been spoiled rotten by my nice neighbour in our absence. They certainly do not look neglected. I put the towels in the wash and switch the coffee machine on.

I take Lloyd's coffee up to him, then sit outside on the bench with my own cup, savouring the lovely feeling of home. The cats jump up on the bench and take their place in my lap and on my shoulder. Yes, Mabel, Lily's cat, seems to think she is a parrot. The dogs normally sit on my lap if I sit down. I'll pick them up later.

I sit and think about last night's discovery. Marilyn and this romantic liaison. It doesn't add up. The silence about it, for one thing. Most girls I've met, and boys too for that matter, can't wait to share news about a possible or actual love interest. I don't think I've met one who's kept it quiet for long. It's such a big thing. So why is this person a secret?

Is he much older? It's the first thought to cross my mind, probably due to my own history: my birth father was more than 20 years older than my birth mother and nowadays would have been called a sexual abuser, a paedophile. My birth mother was just 12 years old when she met him; he was already in his 30s and married with children. Yes, it's not the sort of thing I tend to bring up at dinner parties, but I believe in telling the truth wherever possible.

If people are uncomfortable hearing it then they should try living it. But that was then. This is now, and having sex with children under 16 years is illegal. I just don't think it's someone the same age, because I know children. Why keep him – or her – but knowing a little bit about the way

Marilyn conducts herself, likely a 'him', secret – if there isn't something amiss?

When I bring my coffee cup in I have another read of the card, study the handwriting some more, and take pictures of it and the envelope for evidence. I smile ruefully – being an amateur sleuth seems to be one of the many roles of a foster carer. I rummage in Marilyn's suitcase again and pull out some clothes that I know she didn't wear on holiday. As I lift them out to see if they need a wash, I feel something hard in a pocket.

It's a phone.

I know that on the plane and in the car, and when we stopped off at a service station, she was using the phone with the clean screen-protecting cover. This phone is the other one, with the pulled-up corner of the screen protector.

Why did she hide it?

The battery is flat, which means she will be wanting to charge it. I put it back in the pocket, fold the clothes back up, put them in the suitcase, zip it up again and stand it next to the others. I'll let them all know that I will be putting the residual items in their rooms, which will give her a chance to take the phone. Then I will know for sure that there is something going on.

Jackson comes in with an empty cereal bowl and proceeds to relosd it. I look at his beautifully tanned skin. Normally I would be as dark as he is on returning from holiday. According to the Ancestry DNA tests we did a while back, my heritage is mostly Italian. Jackson and Vincent's DNA results are very different in spite of the fact that they have the same father.

I go upstairs to check on the other children. Vincent is still fast asleep and Lily is sitting up in bed gaming. Normally I'd expect it to be the other way round. I head up to Marilyn's room. I knock quietly on the door and gently open it. I see a pile of blonde hair hanging off the bed, Marilyn is sprawling across the bed, asleep. Her phone is on the side. I notice that the black Nike bag has been pulled out, its contents on display. I step further into the room, as quietly as I can, to get a better look. I bend down cautiously. I see more cards in envelopes. I finger through them and notice that one has our address on. I don't remember it arriving. I see yet another mobile phone, different from the two I know about. A cheap burner phone. I lift the base of the bag up and see cash.

Lots of cash. Shit.

Much, much more cash than an innocent young teenager should have in their bedroom. My heart races.

I know I must report Marilyn's disclosure, but that abuse is historical. She isn't in any danger from her grandfather while she is staying with us and he is miles away. But I think I know what is going on here, and if I'm right, this is far more urgent. I leave everything as I found it and get out of the room quickly. I head straight in to see Lloyd. I explain everything that I've just seen.

We look at each other in alarm. Any trace of the holiday

vanishes (not that I care about that right now) as we go into a state of panic.

'Remember Siobhan?'

'I know. And the scariest bit is that the last card has this address on it. So whoever she's involved with knows where we live.'

XXIV

So much for a gentle start to the day.

As it's a Friday, I know that there isn't a huge amount I can achieve, realistically, before the weekend, but I resolve to start with Moira and get her take on this. I go back out into the garden and call her. It goes straight to the answering machine. *Moira is unable to take your call…*

Of course she is. I leave a message. I emphasise seriousness of what I've just discovered. Because we've been here before.

About five or six years ago we looked after a girl called Siobhan who was a year or two older than Marilyn. She was only here a few weeks because she was heavily involved in County Lines. Putting it like that makes it sound like it was a career choice. It was not.

County Lines, the organised criminal distribution of drugs from the big cities into smaller towns and rural areas using children and vulnerable people, is never a choice. It's a national network of child exploitation and slavery, and

Siobhan was part of it. She had to be moved, not to the other side of the county, but to the other side of the country. That move was not arranged by the police or social services. It was organised by her uncle. He stepped in because Siobhan's parents were both drug users who were also caught up in the gang culture. It was one of the worst experiences of our lives.

We were terrified, not only for her but for our own safety and that of our children. When she came back to this part of the country she was stabbed by another girl in some sort of revenge attack. That girl is in prison and Siobhan has disappeared from the radar. It is a very dangerous situation with devastating consequences.

What I am seeing with Marilyn has the same kind of gang involvement written all over it. The money, the designer gear, the multiple phones, the secrecy.

One of the things I learnt last time was the importance of not just telling one agency and assuming they will communicate effectively with the others. Therefore, I plan to do everything in triplicate: children's social care (all of those who are connected with Marilyn that I have the email of), plus the police and Crimestoppers. Marilyn is not in school at the moment, so I don't have to deal with an education safeguarding team there. Since it's the summer holidays, we wouldn't be talking to them anyway. But this is definitely a matter for the police as well as social services.

The second thing I learnt is that everyone has an agenda.

The police are, like other publicly-funded institutions, under-resourced. This has been exacerbated since the widely-documented cuts of 2015, affecting thousands of frontline officers. Children's social care is similarly under-resourced – and individuals can also be ill-informed.

The final thing I learned from my previous experience is that, as members of the public desperate for someone to treat this with the seriousness it deserves, we will have to gather enough evidence to get get someone to look at the case. It's happening in all walks of life.

As citizens, we're working harder and harder. Just take self-serve checkouts, self-serve restaurants. Translate that to self-service policing.

I go to my office and launch into action on my laptop. I start with the Crimestoppers website. It's a charity and you can post anonymously. They will cross-reference with the police and hopefully acknowledge a crime.

Next I email Moira with a detailed outline of my findings and concerns. I don't know if there is a new social worker for Marilyn yet, so I send Nice Brian a copy of the email.

Initial alerts completed, and next lot of holiday washing hung out, I have a brainwave. I'll call Emily and glean from her what she knows. She doesn't answer her phone but does send a text.

I'll phone you back this afternoon.

Well, that's something. I shower and then head to the shops to buy interim food. I can only think of getting through today. I am nowhere near ready to plan meals, so I opt for a load of easy hot and cold buffet components. Which is code for 'mostly pizza'!

I zip to Sainsbury's car park, leave the car and head into the bakers to get some fresh bread. Then I dash back to the supermarket for five pizzas and a load of dips and Kettle chips. I get some sandwich stuff to keep them going.

As I walk back to the car I see a yellow Mini. It looks a bit like the one I saw before: mustard yellow with black stripes. I make a note of its number plate. I hang back and pretend to look at my phone to buy a bit of time while waiting to see if anyone gets in. I give it 20 minutes then get bored. I don't think I'd be very successful on a stakeout, but then I'm not a trained detective.

I drive home and do my best to forget about mustard-coloured Minis and gangs for the afternoon, until Moira calls me.

'How was the holiday?'

'Not what we expected.'

I explain what a tough time we had out there, and how sometimes we weren't sure how to keep Marilyn safe.

She is sympathetic.

Then I tell her about our concerns for Marilyn.

'Do you have any actual evidence?'

'Well, I've got suspicions about the two phones, and then there's the money and the burner phone in the Nike bag under her bed.'

'Slow down. You're jumping to all sorts of conclusions. This doesn't necessarily mean County Lines, Louise.'

When a social worker reminds me what my name is, I know it means trouble.

'Moira, it doesn't matter if it's County Lines, washing lines or fishing lines. Something is very wrong. Does your daughter have a black Nike bag tucked under her bed with loads of cash and a burner phone and love letters from someone who is more than likely grooming her?'

'Louise, now you're being silly. My daughter is not involved with anything like this.'

I realise that I'm getting cross with her. 'How do you know?'

She has the audacity to say, 'Because I'm her mother.'

My goodness, she's grinding my gears today.

'And while Marilyn is in my care, I'm her bloody mother!'

'Louise, we don't know what she's involved in, or even if she is involved in anything at all.'

'Moira, you're not listening to me. She is 13 years old. She has romantic letters and love tokens and three phones. What do you really think is going on here? Moira?'

Lloyd comes in making a face. It's a face I know well, the one that says, 'Oh no!'

I'm pacing about, unable to listen to Moira properly because nothing I say is getting through. I say, 'Sorry, Moira, someone is at the door!' I hang up and tell Lloyd about her response.

'I guessed as much because I could hear you from upstairs.'

The phone goes again almost immediately. It's Emily.

'Hi Emily, are you okay?'

She is fine and asks how the holiday went. I tell her the truth. She is genuinely sad and apologises. I ask her about the Gucci bag, the phones, the make-up, everything that is not sitting right. Emily confirms that she did not buy her two other phones or the bag.

'But in her other placement, with the old couple, I know that Marilyn was involved with some boys. Older lads.'

I say it. 'Do you think she is involved in County Lines?'

Emily goes quiet for a moment. 'I don't know. I never thought of that. I thought she was messing about with boys and playing up her foster carers.'

'I think it was much more than that. I think we may have a serious problem.'

XXV

I explain carefully what I think is going on, bearing in mind that sometimes talking to and working with parents directly can backfire. I've observed it many times, especially with girls. When girls hit a certain age, often around Year 7 and 8, in my experience, they can become quite challenging, and that's putting it mildly.

There is no question in my mind that phones are part of the problem. And children seem to come with a phone earlier and earlier. My friend, Lyn, is fostering a little boy of just seven years of age who came to the placement with an iPhone, and would not agree to any of her rules about phones. In fact, he became quite violent towards her and her daughter.

Eventually Lyn managed to get hold of the phone by getting the PIN from the boy and found that it was his family had been contacting him and telling him how to break down the placement to get back home. What the family didn't realise was that if the boy did manage to break down the placement, he would almost certainly *not* go back home. Given that there is a national shortage of foster carers, the chances are that if they couldn't find him a placement they would move him out of the area or possibly into residential care. That would be hard for a boy his age. Phones are making it harder and harder to look after children and keep them safe.

At the moment Marilyn hasn't *got* a social worker and Moira is being weird and unhelpful, so frankly, Emily is all I've got. It turns out that Marilyn talks to her mum anyway – but Alan, Emily's partner, doesn't know that.

'So, did Marilyn talk about the holiday?' I ask.

Emily pauses, probably choosing her words carefully. 'Marilyn said you were horrible to her and made her cry.'

'Oh, Emily, that's just not true.' I want to say, 'Your bloody daughter ruined our holiday and nearly caused a divorce', but I don't, because I'm a foster carer and that's not what we do. We quietly seethe while making dinner, doing the washing and reading up on the latest research and social and psychological theories. Doing anything else but inward seething would be deemed as being 'difficult'.

I often think it's a good job no one can hear my thoughts. Before I could say 'kangaroo court' I'd be up in front of the LADO (that's the Local Authority Designated Officer, the person who should be notified when it's been alleged that a professional or volunteer who works with children has behaved in a way that has harmed a child).

I need information from Emily. I want to know more about these older boys. Who they were, how she met them, what she was doing. Grooming is subtle, and one of the easiest ways to groom girls is to tell them that you love them. It makes me so angry that even in the 21st century, girls are hardwired to believe that one day they will be saved, rescued and loved. Publishers and film studios make a fortune from them wanting to believe it. We are failing girls. How many girls grow up hoping and dreaming for that but never get it? Instead we need to teach them that the world is not like that.

But Emily doesn't have any of the answers that I need. She isn't quite sure what was going on and even seems a little laissez-faire about it.

'Do you think you could try to ask Marilyn some probing questions when you're next in contact with her?' I ask. 'To find out about these boys?'

I don't seem to get very far. If I'm honest, Emily sounds a little drunk. For the time being, I'm on my own.

I promise Emily that I'll do my best to keep Marilyn safe. I hope she can't hear how hollow those words sound.

When I check my emails, I see one from someone called Alison. It's Marilyn's new social worker introducing herself. Well, that's something. At least having a social worker is be a step in the right direction. I start to write a reply when my phone goes. It's Alison.

'Hi Louise, I'm Ali and I'll be taking over Marilyn's casework.'

"Casework" always sounds a bit like a police investigation to me. But Alison sounds enthusiastic, if very young. On the phone at least, with her high-pitched voice, she sounds about the same age as Lily. Still, that's a well-documented side effect of getting older – professionals in all walks of life begin to seem impossibly young. I remember someone saying that you know you're getting old when you notice how young police officers are.

Ali arranges to come the next day to meet Marilyn. Blimey, I think the social workers must have had a meeting about Marilyn and the Allens.

Meanwhile, Moira has sent feedback forms for us and the children for our annual review. As someone who genuinely believes in the 'children's voice' I print them off and dish them out at dinner time.

I read their responses and show them to Lloyd. He squints at Vincent's and Jackson's. Vincent's is the most honest, whereas Jackson hasn't bothered to write much at all. His feedback basically amounts to, 'Yeah, it was okay.'

Vincent, on the other hand, has written that Marilyn ruined his holiday, that she self-harmed in front of him and the others, that he wanted to spend more time with me.

Lloyd looks perturbed. 'Should we send that in? I mean they may overreact. You know what they're like.'

I think for a minute or two. 'But that all did happen. And these are his genuine authentic thoughts.' It's tricky. I know what Lloyd means and have seen the repercussions many times. Fostering is built on layers of half-truths born of fear, so no-one ever really knows what's going on. 'I think we *should* tell the truth. It's important that children's social care knows the truth or how else will they improve their work?'

We decide to send it, and the others, back to Moira without intervention.

XXVI

Today we await the visit of Alison. I know nothing about her other than she is Marilyn's newest social worker.

Marilyn is in the kitchen doing some weird art project painting what I can only describe as 'blobs'. Still, if it's allowing her to feel calm and relaxed, then bring on the blobs!I was wise to cover the table with a plastic picnic sheet. She is really going for it and has her hands right in the colourful paints. Her long, beautiful nails are stained with colour, a sight I would much prefer to see on a 13-year-old girl than the perfect manicure she usually sports. While she is enjoying the sensory experience I think of something else to add to the tactile nature of her creative process.

I look in the cupboard and get out the bag of flour. I tip half the bag into a mixing bowl, add salt and fill a mug up with water to gently tip it into the mix. I make enough to divide up into four. I separate out the equal amounts and place them into cereal bowls. I get three bottles of food colouring from the top shelf of the cupboard – red, blue and yellow. I suggest that she keeps one white. She tips a few drops of colour into each bowl and kneads the mixture with her hands. Her face is totally engrossed. She is concentrating hard and this is good news. By doing activities like this we can give our minds a little holiday from all the stress and strains of life.

She looks up at me gratefully. Then smiles and giggles with the new medium. I leave it to her what she wants to make. I fill the water sprayer up and screw on the nozzle so that she can keep the mixtures moist and I pour some spare flour into another cereal bowl in case she wants the mixture to become a bit stiffer. Learning about consistency is great fun and will help Marilyn with both cooking and crafting in the future.

I suddenly realise I've lost track of time. Alison will be here shortly. I run around the house giving the other children a five-minute warning in case they want to grab some snacks and drinks to take upstairs before she arrives. (The strict 'no food in your room' policy goes right out the window when social workers come around. What can I say? The children are the opposite of nosey on these occasions; they seem to just want to hide.)

Time goes past the allotted hour of our appointment time by 15 minutes. I check my phone to see if Alison has been held up. Nothing. I carry on doing what I can, but in limbo, not quite able to settle to anything worthwhile knowing that we are due shortly to have a visitor. I wander into the garden and do a bit of deadheading. The dogs will let me know if there is a knock at the door. At half past the hour I go back in and check my phone again. Still nothing.

I walk past a very happy and content Marilyn, who has her phone next to her but isn't giving it much attention. She is totally absorbed in her artwork, which might not be winning any prizes but is a joy to see. I know Lily and the boys love doing activities like this and, as soon as Alison has gone, they can join in.

I go to my studio to check my emails to see if she's contacted me that way and cancelled or postponed. From the window I see there is a dark blue car parked outside the house. There is a young, blonde, curly-haired woman on the phone. I can only guess that must be Alison.

Well, that's rude!

After another five minutes, the knock at the door finally comes. The dogs run up to the door to see who is there. I open the door to a young woman in a pale blue denim jacket over a summer dress, wearing white pumps. She has pink and purple streaks at the front of her hair, framing her face. I greet her politely but cannot resist asking, 'Was there bad traffic?'

She has the good grace to blush. 'Sorry, no. It wasn't traffic. My manager wanted to talk to me.' I'm suddenly struck by a feeling that her blushes cover something more than embarrassment at arriving more than half an hour late. I don't know why, quite, but I do have good instinct and I just feel like something is cooking in the background here.

I invite Alison into the kitchen, where Marilyn is still sitting at the table. She looks up from her blobs and smiles. I wonder what the age difference is between them.

Alison smiles again at Marilyn and then speaks. 'Hi Marilyn. I'm Ali. Did Louise tell you I was coming?'

What a stupid question. Of course I did.

Some social workers have the knack of winding up foster carers and children. It's often only small things, but they add up and make you feel uncomfortable around that person. I suspect it's because they simply don't think. Ali is definitely falling into this category already.

I'm the grown-up in the room. Looking at Ali, I feel pretty certain about that. Is it because I'm getting older? I shake my head and have that thought about police officers seeming younger again. Ali seems nice enough, and I will let that little comment go; I shall put it down to her newness.

Ali sits down in front of Marilyn. Again I find myself being judgemental. Another age and experience observation, but it would be less imposing to sit alongside, or not quite in front of Marilyn. Maybe the next seat along would not threaten her as much. I can tell from her body language that she is beginning to feel that sense of threat. When a child feels threatened, especially one who has experienced trauma, they tend not to behave as well as they could. They feel defensive and scared and use the bravado of being loud and lairy to protect themselves.

Ali settles into her seat and pulls out her laptop. Oh dear.

I know I'm being hyper-critical now, but this is not good. She should have waited before getting the laptop out. Or perhaps not used it at all. It comes across as another little power play, even if it isn't intended that way.

Start slowly, I think. Social workers have an hour or two in their diary and sometimes they think that they have to use it. My approach would have been more along the lines of, 'Hi Marilyn, I thought I'd come and say hello.' Totally unthreatening and Marilyn would not have minded. When I read Marilyn's referral, and after chatting to her a little, I think it's safe to say that she has had a fair few social workers in her time. After a while, a child will get fed-up with another new face. I imagine it's probably even more frustrating than foster carers having to meet new supervising social workers and start all over again.

'Right, well. Ali, would you like a cup of tea or coffee, or perhaps a cold drink?'

She asks for a coffee, 'with oat milk if you have it'.

I do, actually. Lloyd's daughter and her boyfriend were meant to be coming over at the weekend but cancelled. They are both vegans so I made sure I had plenty of oat milk and other plant-based products when they're due. Ha!

'Coming right up!' I don't tell her that in her line of work she might want to adjust her preferences. I busy myself in the kitchen while Ali tries to communicate with a reluctant Marilyn. As a woman, it never ceases to amaze me how quickly we become invisible in a domestic situation, which is why cleaners make the best spies. Or should I say why spies pretend to be cleaners? That's a better description, or most cleaners would need to speak Russian and have a good degree from Oxford to secure their cleaning positions. I ponder on such nonsense but turn around when I hear the squirting sound of the water spray.

Marilyn is holding it up in front of Ali, who is, daftly, sitting right opposite her, like a gun to her head, spraying it into her face. This is weird. I don't imagine for one moment that it's a role play that Ali will have been through on her social work course. But perhaps she should have been taught that sitting directly opposite a frightened child is not a good idea.

Since Ali doesn't seem to know how to react, it is left to me. 'Marilyn, stop that and put the spray down.'

This could have been the simple end of it; but no, Ali says, 'It's okay, Louise. If Marilyn feels that she wants to do this, that's fine. It's all about building trust.'

I move behind Ali, pretending to head for the cupboard, and look at Marilyn, who catches my eye with a smirk. I throw her a 'put down your weapon' face. It's not that easy to describe. You really have to see it. Foster carers, the police and headteachers can do this face at will.

Marilyn puts down the spray and pretends to listen to Ali.

I present Ali with a large mug of coffee with oat milk.

'How about you, Marilyn? Would you like a drink?' Looking at her hands

I also ask if she would like to wash them. I get two straight 'no's in reply. Well, at least that's clear.

'Louise, can I be alone with Marilyn for a few moments?'

What? I am incensed and concerned. What the hell does she think she is doing? She's only just met Marilyn and now she wants Marilyn to confide in her. She has asked me to leave my own kitchen? I smile (and seethe inwardly) and head out to the hall, where I realise that I literally don't know what to do.

I walk along to Lloyd's studio, where he is quietly working on something involved and technical.

'I can't believe that bloody social worker!'

He nods and makes a 'hmm' sound.

'You won't believe what she said!'

Lloyd holds up his hand to 'sshh' me, and I'm just about to be incensed all over again. Then he whispers, 'I *did* hear. Listen'.

He points towards his top window that goes into the conservatory, which is built onto the kitchen. It's wide open.

Ali is asking Marilyn if she self-injured in front of the children. 'Vincent, perhaps?'

I'm listening intently now as this is evidently about Vincent's feedback. I knew there was a different agenda today. She is asking Marilyn what happened on holiday which we clearly wrote about in the feedback. I suspect this is not about Marilyn and her wellbeing. Surely the fact that she self-harmed is not the primary issue. What about the disclosure about her grandfather? What about the fact that she might be in immediate danger from her involvement in County Lines?

Nor is this about our welfare, for that matter. This is not about keeping us safe from drug gangs. I suspect this is about culpability and who to blame. They were not interested in doing a risk assessment. In my head, I quickly run through all the emails I sent to Freda, Moira and Brian when Marilyn first arrived. I raised concerns about the holiday many times and asked for a risk assessment that never happened. I think Vincent's honest feedback got their attention and I'm sure the priority now is to protect themselves, not Marilyn or us.

Experience has taught me that this is not good.

Fed-up with not being allowed in my own kitchen, I decide to return. It's my house, after all. Ali is sitting at the table, staring down the barrel of a water nozzle. Her hair and clothes are soaking wet. The water spray embargo obviously didn't last long.

'Can you go now, please?' Marilyn asks Ali. Her tone makes it clear that this is not a request.. Woah, the power of a 13-year-old girl is amazing. I'm quite proud of her.

I waft in and ask Ali if she would like another coffee. I'm perfectly polite as I have a suspicion that everything I say and do will be taken down and used in evidence against me.

Where is Moira when I need her? Actually, when I reflect, Moira hasn't said or done anything useful surrounding Marilyn, before, during or after the holiday. She knows we had a difficult holiday because I submitted my diary of the two weeks, but she didn't comment. I reckon they're worried. Maybe they've got an Ofsted inspection coming up, or someone somewhere has broken the rules.

Ali declines the offer of coffee and makes her soggy way out of my house. I am uneasy about the whole encounter. We have got nowhere with the real issue here: my County Lines concerns.

XXVII

It's a horrible feeling when you think you're being investigated, or worse, being set up.

Marilyn has plunged her hands back in the blobs, swirling her fingers around with renewed determination.

'Are you okay?'

She nods. 'I didn't like her.'

I smile. Nor did I. I leave her to it, then I do a quick swoop around the upper floors to see if the others are alright. They want to know if the woman is gone because they're 'starving', apparently.

I go into my studio and pull up all the emails I have sent and received since we met Marilyn, and the few before. I scan them quickly. Enough to reassure myself that I have mentioned every concern I had, from risk assessments, to the unsuitability of the required change in holiday accommodation, through to payments and funding. Everything is in the emails, as I was certain it would be, but Ali's visit has left me feeling vulnerable and questioning myself. I find one where I first mention self-harming or, as the younger social workers say, 'self-injury'.

They *must* be checking with Marilyn because of the feedback from Vincent – and Lily, who was quite honest too. Jackson went for the path of least resistance, and I still suspect that was because he basically couldn't be bothered. Something has set my teeth on edge and I can't quite put my finger on it. We have been here many times before. I know that something is brewing. I pop my head around Lloyd's office door and explain my concerns.

'Absolutely. We *did* raise all our concerns before we went. We were very clear that we had plenty of concerns. Neither of us was keen to do it, if you recall.' Then he shrugs his shoulders. 'Don't worry about it.'

But I do worry about it. So much that I find myself checking with the National Union of Professional Foster Carers (NUPFC) that we have not done anything wrong. They confirm that risk assessments should have been done, and in fact, explain that it sounds as if we were 'coerced' into taking Marilyn with us. Thinking back, it was a form of coercion. It certainly felt as if there was no way of refusing.

The rest of the day passes and Marilyn seems quite relaxed, despite the visit from Ali, who, in my opinion, needs to go back to school and learn a little more emotional intelligence. As much for her own sake as for those she is responsible for. It's the same for foster carers, though. It's the little things that matter. Picking up on them early and recognising that something may be brewing is an art that we need to learn fast. Nipping things in the bud is always the safest approach to working and living with children who have experienced trauma. Actually, when I think about it, that applies to all children, not just those recovering from trauma.

Lily and Jackson cannot resist picking up where Marilyn left off with the art project. They are especially interested in the homemade clay, or playdough; the word I choose depends on the audience. I love watching children when they are engrossed in something. They always look amazing and real. Their faces become countenances of innocence again, all traces of posturing and adult mannerisms evaporate when they are absorbed in something good.

We have a couple of nice weather days. I take all the children for drives to the countryside or the beaches with picnics and dogs. Marilyn seems okay, even though the phone does ping a lot. Once again she seems to alternate between the smooth one and the one with the curled-up screen protector. I'm very conscious of the switch between them, but can't work out a pattern. She has her Gucci bag with her all the time and never brings out both at the same time.

On the third day she asks if she could go into town tomorrow. A normal request under ordinary circumstances, but the alarm bells are already ringing.

'Why? What do you need? And who are you going to go with?'

She is cagey but, after a few pings of the phone, she asks if she can go with Lily.

This makes me feel a bit better as Lily is a sensible girl. We put the Find My Friends app on all the phones a while ago. That obviously doesn't apply to Marilyn's phone(s) since we can't get anywhere near them. I agree and tell Lloyd so that plans are discussed very clearly and openly.

The next day the girls get ready to go into town. They have very different approaches to this. For Lily that means changing her hoodie. For Marilyn it involves three hours preparing herself, including a spray tan and hair toner. This time her hair goes a sort of mauve. I'm not sure if that is the look that she is going for, because she reapplies it. By the time she's finished she has a white hoodie and shorts, violet hair, orange face and legs, white trainers and her Gucci bag. That's an awful lot of effort to go into town which, if you know our local area, isn't too exciting.

The boys are doing something that they don't seem to do so much these days: hanging out together. They are in the back garden setting up badminton and other activities. Ages ago I bought some cheap stopwatches to help with a child we were looking after who was very overweight but competitive. I set up loads of challenges that seemed to help shed some of the weight. I was warmed to see the boys outside laughing and beating each other up (in a friendly way).

Meanwhile, the girls present themselves to me in the kitchen. Lloyd walks in, looking for a phone charger. (They seem to get up and walk off by themselves in this house.) He raises his eyebrows at Marilyn's attire. I think it's more at the orangeness of her skin than the shortness of her shorts. I hadn't previously noticed the stuck-on pale pink talons. They look awful, but I take my usual position: it's her show.

'Right then, you two,' I say in front of Lloyd, so there can be no question about the arrangements. 'You know you have to be back by 6pm. That isn't 6.05pm, or even 6.01pm. That is six o'clock on the dot.'

They both pull faces but the truth is that in this town they will be done with the things that are suitable for them within two hours at a push. So any longer and I would be wondering where they are. Lily probably hasn't a clue that we put the app on her phone. We did tell her about two years ago but I'm sure that she wasn't listening and we haven't had much cause to use it.

Off they go. The day goes by. It's nice that the boys are bonding again after the holiday debacle and the girls are out doing 'girl things'. All the same, it isn't long before I ask Lloyd to have a look on his phone and see where Lily is.

'She's at the leisure centre.'

'The leisure centre? Did they mention that? I think I'll just text her to see how she is doing.'

I'm aware that could be construed as a little overprotective, but that's my nature. It's partly to do with being a foster carer. We tend to have a heightened sense of worry, and this is then exacerbated by fretting over whether we are too protective or not protective enough. It's partly instinctive and partly institutional. Giving too much freedom, or not enough, is a concern for every parent – but we foster carers have our our parent choices questioned, judged and analysed continuously. So, of course, we tend to overthink things and sometimes, even worse, lose our confidence in our own decision-making abilities.

My fallback position is always to consider what I would do for my birth children. No matter how hard I try to treat foster children as my own, it is always hard – especially when there are birth parents and social workers on the scene. But, as a mother and as a woman, I am fearful for girls in particular. It can be tough, sometimes, just walking along the road. Lily was very upset recently when she was in town with her best friend, Ruby. A group of young men shouted out to them, 'I'd give 'er one!'

The absolute ridiculousness of everything about that statement is too much to bear and is one of the (many) things that makes being a female hard work. A great deal of our existence is treacherous. As one of my old flames said one evening under the influence of a lot of wine, 'Women are clearly the far greater sex. The only thing Mother Nature got wrong was making most men bigger and stronger.' A good observation, ahead of its time. Or maybe he was doing what some men do, say the thing he imagined I wanted to hear.

While I'm working myself up thinking about all

this, Lloyd says, 'They've moved. Look. She's now in the supermarket car park.'

My hackles are up. Those alarm bells are ringing loud and long.

'Right. In that case, can I borrow your car?'

Lily and Marilyn would instantly recognise mine. It's the one we most often use and it's distinctive. Lloyd's is white and less easy to distinguish. I wear sunglasses and grab Vincent's baseball cap on the way out. I'm well aware that I'm not going to win this year's Best Secret Agent award, should there be such a thing, but it's the best I can do in the moment.

Because my car is an automatic and I'm not used to driving Lloyd's, I have to remind myself how to use the gears. I catch a glimpse of myself in the mirror and it strikes me that I look like a drug dealer. A middle-aged, female one, but I reckon I could pull it off.

I reverse Lloyd's car, feeling a bit like I'm in an episode of *Starsky and Hutch*, and zoom up the road. I say 'zoom', but I remain well within the speed limit – foster carers need their licences. I head straight to the car park and spot the girls with those boys again. A plethora of grey tracksuit bottoms and the 'roadman' bags. Lily, I notice immediately, looks decidedly ill at ease.

I reverse into a parking space under a tree and watch.

After a few minutes, I text Lily. *Hi darling, are you okay?*

She texts straight back. *Yeah, I'm fine.*

I can see that she's not. Marilyn is all Ali G and moving in a performative way, like girls do when they want to be noticed. Not Lily. The boys are on electric scooters and bikes. I can't stand watching Lily looking this down in the mouth, and I'm curious about Marilyn. She does not behave like this at home, nor did she when we were on holiday.

Hang on, there's that mustard-yellow Mini.

I watch carefully. It drives by the group of young people. Marilyn opens the door and seems to be encouraging Lily to get in. I turn on the engine and, at speed, drive around the car park the wrong way too fast. I slow down and beep the horn so that Lily sees me. I fly out of the car, walk straight towards Lily and Marilyn and call out, 'Dinner time, darlings!' It's far too early for dinner, but I don't know what else to say.

Inside the mustard Mini are two older boys in the front in black hoodies, more expensive attire. I look right at them. 'Hello there, how are you? I'm afraid my girls have to come home for their tea. Come on you two,' I say, turning back to Lily and Marilyn. 'In you get. Don't want to let it get cold now!'

They comply without a word.

The boys in the Mini call me a 'fucking twat' and shoot off.

I turn to the other boys gathered in the car park. I recognise some of them. They used to go to one of the local primary schools where an old friend of mine worked in admin. I remember doing an art session with a few of them.

They were good kids. I look at them and say, for all the good it will do, 'Boys, you need to stop this. You will get hurt.'

I climb back in my car and realise that I'm shaking like a leaf. I drive over to a space on the far side of the car park and turn off the engine.

'Okay. Tell me. Are you both okay?'

Even though Marilyn is, on the surface, behaving a bit like a trollop, the reality is that she is only 13 years old.

They don't answer. I turn around and sigh, 'What was happening there, girls?'

Marilyn is shaking and crying, chewing her nails and reading her phone. Lily is upset and looks scared too. I decide to drive to the police station. We park up and walk to the front. I see the 'closed' sign and read the opening times on the door. They are open Tuesday, Wednesday, Thursday only, 10-4pm. It's Friday. Apparently no crimes are ever committed on a Friday.

I get back in the car, feeling utterly helpless and scared. I ask Marilyn if those boys are messaging her.

She nods, miserably. 'I'm in trouble.'

But she won't say any more.

Are we talking about County Lines and child exploitation? Enraged, I head back to the supermarket car park. The yellow car is there. Bravado evaporates. I change my mind and decide to report what happened to the police.

In the car, I try to change the subject. I know that a hysterical foster carer will not achieve anything other than to silence them – and possibly push them further towards the gang. I take a deep breath and think.

XVIII

After I have settled Marilyn and Lily – and myself – down at home, I tell Lloyd what has happened. His face tightens because we both know what this could mean. Memories of Siobhan, the foster child involved in County Lines, resurface. I've been seeing signs for a while and when I've checked in with social services and Emily, Marilyn's mum, there hasn't been much response. That also concerns me.

I feel on fire with rage and fear. These are young children we are talking about and they can be coerced, manipulated and hurt. It doesn't take long for a child to get into debt-bondage, where a real or perceived debt is used to control them. Often they will be too scared to say anything to the people that they love and that can help them. The last experience we had of County Lines nearly broke me. It was a long time ago, perhaps 10 years or so, and it seems nothing has changed. It isn't just Marilyn – and perhaps now Lily. I have just seen boys who were at primary school not so long ago caught up in whatever is going on here. What to do? Where to start?

I go into my studio intending to email Ali and Moira. Instead I discover they have already emailed me and sent copies to their managers. I stop when I see the first few words: *It is with regret...*

'Lloyd? Lloyd!'

He comes into my studio a few seconds later with a freshly filled bottle of water. I turn my laptop round for him to see.

> *It is with regret that we inform you that you have been suspended from fostering. After a professionals' meeting to discuss the feedback from you and your family, we have decided that you will remain suspended until you have completed the following training:*
> * *De-escalation techniques (3 days)*
> * *Conscious parenting (12 weeks)*
> *Please see the links below for details about how to access these courses...*

The email goes on, but I've read enough. I'm speechless. But not for long. I call Moira, who actually answers. I remain polite and calm, conscious that a foster friend of mine told me recently that she was cross on the phone but her call was recorded and then she received an allegation as a result.

Lloyd is furious, bringing a visual representation to the description of being 'hopping mad'. I try to wave his anger down while I speak in a measured way into the receiver, 'Hi Moira, it's Louise.'

I balance this with making a 'sshh' finger against my lips and switch to speaker phone.

'How are you?' I continue. (I actually don't care, and don't give her time to reply.)

'We've received your email, thank you. (I don't know why I'm thanking her for this bullshit, but there we are.) 'Do you mind if I just confirm, does "being suspended" mean you are taking our foster children away?'

Her response doesn't surprise me in the slightest. 'No, Louise. What it means is that you cannot foster any *more* children.'

'Moira,' I say, (and I think I probably deserve an Oscar for my ability to continue the performance of calm at this point), 'that's a bit strange, don't you think? Because you know we *can't* foster any more children anyway at this point. We are up to capacity with two. One more, as you know, would take us over our agreed numbers.' I pause. 'So, if this suspension makes no difference to our situation, then why, exactly have you suspended us? What does it actually achieve?'

Lloyd is livid. The whole thing is utterly ridiculous. I know that if an allegation like this is deemed serious then Social Services would take the children away. But of course, that just creates more of a problem for them. I remember that I've already checked with the fostering union that we are not in the wrong, and indeed were coerced into taking Marilyn along with us on holiday, which ended up costing us a great deal more money. That thought helpfully reminds me I still need to get the money back.

'By the way, Moira, we need to claim all the costs back from taking Marilyn on holiday.'

'I'm afraid that you can't. If you refer to the Foster Carers' Handbook, you will see that you are entitled to £60 per week extra holiday allowance.'

Now we both know that this is a complete con and we have been done, and if they admit to anything, that will give us leverage. They must be worried, because the way that Moira is talking she is absolutely not herself. It makes me think that they have taken legal advice. I noticed a while ago on LinkedIn that most senior managers these days have done a law degree. Perhaps that's to protect themselves, rather than the children or foster carers.

'Okay, thanks for letting us know,' I say, breezily. 'Oh, one more thing, Moira, while I've got you on the line.'

'Yes?'

'Do look out for my next email, won't you? I'm in the process of reporting to the police that Marilyn is connected to County Lines.'

Her response amazes me yet again. 'Louise, we've been through this. You don't know that.'

I take a deep breath. 'Yes, I do, Moira. I had to rescue Lily and Marilyn from a car park where Lily was just about to get in a car with two gang members. I'll inform Lily's social worker, of course.'

Moira goes quiet for a moment. 'Okay. Thanks, Louise.'

I'm doing it to her, too, overusing her name, but every time a social worker uses my name like that I know that they are somehow trying to assert authority and pull rank. She will have to try a lot harder than that.

I do exactly what I said I'd do and email Lily's social worker. She is a lovely woman and we've built up a good relationship over the years. She is from a different office and I know she will act. I get back to the NUPFC and the police, and Crimewatch, who have a section on their charity Facebook page dedicated to reporting incidents that could be related to County Lines and child exploitation.

Three days later, Marilyn is abducted.

XXIX

It's mid-afternoon and I'm whizzing up some flapjacks so there is something warm and gooey for the children to tuck into this afternoon. Feeding them during the holidays gets expensive and some good old-fashioned baking seems to go further and have more appeal than a packet of supermarket biscuits.

The boys have gone to the cinema to see something involving Marvel superheroes, taking advantage of the cheaper early showing. Lily is upstairs in her room 'listening to music'. I could make some jokes about the fact that it doesn't sound like music, and it's so loud there is very little listening going on, but that would make me sound old. Lily seems to have made the decision to stay out of Marilyn's way. I think the car park shenanigans have frightened her. She knows she was out of her depth. Marilyn invents ever more elaborate excuses to leave the house and I find ways to keep her here, explaining that, given what's happened, it isn't safe for her to be out alone. Still, Marilyn's phone, or one of them, vibrates with alerts incessantly.

'Can't you turn the notifications off?'

She shakes her head.

My syrupy, oaty mixture is ready, but the oven is still warming up.

'Here. Spread this out on the tray, will you?' I say, to give her something to do. 'I'm just going to check on my emails.'

Still no movement from anyone in authority. Still no support for Marilyn. An Independent Reviewing Officer, or IRO, called Elizabeth has been appointed to the case. Big deal. Still no-one seems to be taking any of my claims seriously. I know I can't keep Marilyn at home forever. But if I let her out, who knows what will happen? I wander back to the kitchen. Marilyn is nowhere to be seen. The wooden spoon is standing up in the bowl, golden mixture half-spread into the baking tin beside it.

'Marilyn?'

The back door is ajar. I race towards it. Marilyn is at the bottom of the garden, struggling between two figures in hoodies.

'Marilyn!'

I know I'm not going to be a match for anyone that age, and who knows what they might be carrying?

I run back to the kitchen and call the emergency services. By the time I reach the end of the garden I see a silver Mini disappearing into the distance. It's too far for me to catch the registration in full. I think it's a 57 plate, so a good few years old. There might be an 'F' or a 'K'. Damn my eyesight.

I pass on all the information I can, for what it's worth.

We have a hellish few hours. I can't believe she's gone – in broad daylight, from my house. It's terrifying. I don't know how deeply she has got herself into this, and I have no idea how it might end. I'm also desperately frightened for my family. If there was ever any doubt that 'they', whoever 'they' are, know where we live, that has been removed.

The evening is grim while we wait for news. I finish the flapjacks at some point, but not even VIncent and Jackson have the appetite for them.

When it gets to midnight I send everyone else to bed. 'There's no point in us all waiting up. Off you go.'

Lloyd and the children troop off. I sit in silence at the kitchen table, beside myself with worry. It's nearly 2am when I receive the call to say that she has been found and that she is okay.

'Thank God.' I feel sick with relief. The police are going to bring her back. I move to the sitting room, worried that I might not hear them when they arrive. I anticipate them being quiet in a residential street at this time of night, but when they eventually turn up, closer to 4am, it sounds like we are being raided. I'll deal with the neighbours tomorrow.

I send Marilyn to bed within 15 minutes of her return and make the police officers tea. They are very happy to sit down and drink it. They've driven for two hours from another county, where Marilyn had been taken to a trap house. They can't give me all the details because of the nature of an ongoing investigation.

'But there have been a number of arrests,' one of the officers assures me.

'And Marilyn was not the only girl there,' the other one adds.

'So it was County Lines?'

'Oh, yes.'

It turns out that not only is Marilyn heavily involved in County Lines, she has been for years. And it was known about.

'It wasn't on the bloody referral,' I mutter.

'Would you have taken her if it was?' The officer's voice is gentle.

I still can't believe that they chose not to tell us. And no wonder they were so keen to get her out of the country on holiday with us – it meant she wasn't accessible for a couple of weeks. But I'm livid.

'To be honest, I've struggled to get the social workers to listen to me, even after I worked out that Marilyn was involved with County Lines.' I explain about the phones and the bag of cash and the car park.

They aren't surprised. 'We hear this all the time.'

'But what am I supposed to do? How am I supposed to look after her? I can't take this responsibility. And I'm endangering my own family.'

They tell me that they will be pushing for Marilyn to be

taken to a safe and secure place. They have already spoken to Elizabeth, the IRO, who, in their words, is 'not impressed' with what has happened.

The hours that Marilyn was gone were hellish. But her abduction did have one good outcome – they're finally taking us seriously.

XXX

It is Elizabeth, the Independent Reviewing Officer, who does the right thing in the end. She uses what powers she has to remove Marilyn from our home, to protect her and us. It happens just two days after the police return her to our house following the abduction.

Alison, 'call-me-Ali', the new social worker, and Carole, her manager, arrive to collect Marilyn. The last few days have been quiet but emotional for all of us.

While Ali helps pack Marilyn's stuff, Carole accuses Lloyd and me of neglect and failing to ensure Marilyn's safety.

I am simply not in the mood for any more bullshit. I let her bully us and let her say all that she has planned to say to demoralise us and shift the blame on to us. It washes over me. It's easier than trying to fight back.

Dotty is not impressed with Carole either. She keeps coming back into the kitchen to bark at her.

'Can you get that dog out?' she says.

I rise from my chair in the kitchen. 'No, I can't. But you can get out of my house and go and wait in your car.'

As an ex-care-system kid I have certain skills – and certain reactions – that sometimes take me by surprise. I move a few inches forward and silently point in the direction of the hall.

Carole gets up to leave.

I go upstairs to check on Marilyn. I find her collapsed on the floor, crying.

'I don't want to go.'

We've spoken at length about why it is impossible for her to stay with us, and she understands that it will be the best thing in the long run. That doesn't make it any easier. Alison has her arm around her and is crying too.

'Why don't you both go downstairs?' I say gently. 'Lloyd will make you a hot drink and I'll do this bit.'

Ali is so young for this role, perhaps in her very early 20s. I can see she is hurting very much at how this – one of her first cases – has all turned out. I don't think any of it is her fault. She is actually very kind, and I can see her going on to be a good social worker – if she ignores some of the models set by her senior and supposedly 'superior' managers.

'As long as you feel children like Marilyn's pain and work hard to help them, you will be a good social worker,' I try to reassure her.

She nods.

'I've sent Carole out to wait in her car. I'd had enough of her.' I wink at her.

The time I see Marilyn, she is holding the grey fluffy teddy with the big love heart, crying as she walks out the door with Ali. I put Marilyn's bags outside, which include the suitcase we got her for the holiday, and leave them on the step.

I approach Carole's car and knock on the window. 'The bags are on the step.'

I go back inside, then quickly run to the sitting room with Lloyd to watch from the window as Carole lugs the bags to her car.

Childish, perhaps. But we are entitled to a little fun.

Epilogue

Every year there is an award ceremony in a large hall for all the children and young people whose social workers have put their names forward. Lily has been put forward to receive prizes. We drive to the big hall, which is on an industrial estate. I have bought Lily and Shannon, our latest foster child, new outfits. Shannon is up for an award, too. She wanted to take her scooter – which, of course, I let her do.

I always appreciate the effort that goes into these events. Our attendance has been very regular. Lily has received a prize every year and is now of the view that children, even her, receive prizes 'just for breathing'.

A little cynical, perhaps, but I see her point. Lily is up for a prize in the Academic Achievement category. All councils are desperate to demonstrate that children in care can do well at school. Lily generally does well because she is bright and hardworking and we have made a real effort to build her self-esteem and confidence.

Though Year 8, it's true, is rather different. It seems to be the year that children in care are more likely to plummet academically, and to start to fall by the wayside in school. Foster carers need nerves of steel, and the child's stability and success depend on the quality of support around the child and foster family. I see signs that Lily could indeed wander off down a different path, but we just hope that we have instilled in her as much sense and love as possible.

Shannon has been with us for four months now. She is a poppet, at the same time as being a bit wild. We took an enforced six-month break after Marilyn left. Initially, we had been suspended from looking after any more children, even though we were still currently looking after two foster children and were up to our agreed limit.

We felt that the decision was an act of punishment and self-protectionism by a few of the managers because they had failed to be honest and do risk assessments.

After Marilyn left we were worn out.

Moira used that as the new reason why we were suspended. I was outspoken at that point, and emailed the Independent Investigator with my thoughts and evidence. As any foster carer will know, it is rare that we win because they operate together and, as far as I am concerned, no-one is 'independent' if they are on the same payroll. I have heard of Independents speaking up but they are never asked back.

After Marilyn left we were quite broke, financially. We lost the allowance and could not foster another child because of the suspension. We, mainly me, had paid for all the holiday and added costs for Marilyn. They never let me reclaim the money. It was a difficult time.

I spoke to Emily one more time and sent her the grandparents' information that was lent to me in order to get Marilyn's passport. We continued to argue and stand our ground with the social work managers. It was a bitter end.

Shannon is a lovely girl, but hard work. We are working hard with the school to write an EHCP (Education, Health and Care Plan). Like so many others, she should already have had one, but she wasn't at the last two schools she attended long enough for them to gather the evidence and get it written. She needs an educational psychologist review because we, and the school, think she has some specific learning needs.

To be honest, Lloyd and I are tired, tired of the uphill battles we have every day to try to keep children safe and meet their needs and I'm fed up with merely 'meeting their needs'. I'm fed up that this has become the only expectation for us and the children. I want to be aspirational for them but, my word, it's becoming hard. More and more foster carers are leaving because they reckon it just isn't worth it.

But what about the increasing numbers of children coming into care?

I try to push all these thoughts aside as I park, retrieve Shannon's scooter from the boot of the car, and walk into the hall. Shannon insists on riding her scooter right into the building. I smile to myself as I see some of the social workers dodge out of her way. We are greeted by the assistant social workers, who make a huge fuss of all the children and young people walking up the red carpet.

The foster carers and children take seats at the tables. There are games and fun things to do. It's a bit like Pizza Hut in the '90s. I wave at my fellow foster carers and share the same promises. 'We must catch up soon. I have loads to tell you.'

We don't often get together, but we are all conscious that this event is for the children. As the speeches start and the children quickly become restless, I look around the room. In many ways, important as they are, I think these events sum up some of what is wrong with fostering, why so many carers are leaving, and why there is difficulty recruiting new ones. I take the rubbish pay out of it and study the room.

At the very back are the senior managers. These are the women with the nicest handbags, the men in suits and Disney socks. They watch everyone else, all of us. The sides of the room are lined with social workers, also watching us. The assistants run around sorting out the mock cocktails and buffet.

It's hideous, and belies a hierarchical system.

Those near the top of the hierarchy believe that they are better and do not mix with those at the bottom of the pile. What a terribly draconian set-up it is, and represents the way in which the 'them and us' battlelines are so firmly drawn into the ground. I feel more and more despondent all the time. I look back at Lily and Shannon, the reasons we are here. Shannon can't keep still. I take her outside to the garden area to burn off some energy. I walk past a few tables and see lots of teenagers. Because it's organised in age categories, they have to wait a long time to receive their awards. There are over a hundred children to get through.

I stand outside and watch Shannon zoom backwards and forwards. I know Lily will be fine. She is sitting next to a fellow foster carer with a child she knows from school. The big fire doors are open. I can see into the room to keep an eye on Lily while watching Shannon at the same time.

The table of teenagers stirs and they begin moving about. They probably want to eat the buffet which is in another room, likely being guarded until the speeches are over.

I hear Lily's name called out, so I call Shannon and take the scooter off her as she comes into the room. We quickly sit back down at our table. Lily is bright red in the face as she walks awkwardly towards the stage. She looks at me and I wave at her and clap. I look for her social worker. I can't see her, but I'm not worried. I know she'll get here. She normally turns up late. Not because she's a bad timekeeper, but because she's usually fire-fighting a tricky situation.

Lily returns to the table, flushed and smiling. I rub her arm, as does the foster carer next to her. Suddenly, out of nowhere, Lily's social worker appears.

'Well done, Lily. We're all very proud of you.'

In a healthy, normal setting, that would be seen as the

right thing to do, but I notice her colleagues and bosses are watching her with something approaching disdain. How weird!

The next category is 'Determination' and this time Shannon's name is called. She is thrilled and almost runs to the stage area where she walks along a line of people. Nobody seems to have told us who they are; perhaps they forgot. I guess they have something to do with fostering. Shannon runs back to her seat, clutching her certificate and beaming. I see her social worker by the wall. She looks over and waves. I point her out to Shannon, who jumps up and, with her award clasped in her hand, runs over to show off her award.

That's really sweet.

I will have to break it to Shannon soon that her social worker is leaving in another month, but not today. After all the speeches are done, proud foster carers and children head towards the buffet. The girls are excited. Who doesn't like a buffet? And they always do a good spread.

'Go on in, girls. I'm just running to the Ladies.'

My fellow foster carer gathers them up as I head to the toilets. In the corridor, I'm approached by a young woman.

'Excuse me, are you Louise?'

'Yes,' I say, wondering if I should recognise this person.

'You don't know me, but I'm Marilyn's key worker. She's over there and wondered if she could say hello.'

I look over, but only see a girl with long brown hair

wearing a loose, checked shirt and jeans. I look around for Marilyn. The girl waves. She *is* Marilyn! But a very different Marilyn to the one we knew.

I walk up to her and hold out my arms as she comes in for a hug. What a lot we shared in just a few short weeks. She is crying and smiling at the same time.

I touch her hair. 'I love this, Marilyn. It really suits you. You look beautiful.'

She sniffs and snorts. 'I feel safer, Louise, looking like this.' She wears no make-up and there is no sign of the orange tan. I hug her again.

'I want to hear all about what's been going on, but I absolutely must go to the loo first, or I'll burst.'

She giggles.

'Will you come and see me after, at our table?'

'Try stopping me!'

As I turn to go to the loo, the key worker says, 'I need the loo too.' We head into the toilets together. While we are washing our hands, I thank her for approaching me and say how wonderful it is to see Marilyn again. Her name is Kirsty and she works at a private residential home for girls. She looks very young (as so many seem to), and is one of the people on the table by the fire doors. They must all be girls from the home with their key workers.

'I'll never forget Marilyn. Partly because we had such a hard time with her.' I tell Kirsty a little bit about how Marilyn was involved in County Lines.

'I know. Marilyn was being used as a procurer to recruit other girls.'

I remember her 'friend' Charlotte, and what might have happened with Lily.

'But she's doing really well now. She attends the home's own school where there are nine girls and she is flourishing. She just received an award for working hard.'

My eyes well up.

While we're drying our hands on the paper towels another woman comes out of one of the cubicles. It's Alison. She talks to me in the mirror.

'Isn't Marilyn doing well?'

I hear that she is still Marilyn's social worker and, like Kirsty, she is full of nothing but praise. 'In separate news, you might also like to know that soon after Marilyn left, Carole left the department too.'

I sense that there is a little more to Alison's statement. I squint and lean into the two young women. 'What was really going on there?'

Alison shrugs.

Kirsty speaks. 'They weren't dealing with the County Lines problem. We've got three other girls who were also involved. It's incompetence.'

Alison looks under the doors in the toilet for feet. 'There's still an ongoing investigation but I don't know if we will ever know the outcome.'

Each of us knows we have said too much, and without

any discussion we leave the toilet separately. I can't help but wonder how many looked-after children who are here have been involved in County Lines. I join the girls in the buffet room. I must admit, my tummy is growling.

I load my plate up, disappointingly, mostly hummus sandwiches, because the locusts have been in. I think about the room next door where all the staff and managers are. I wonder what's really going on.

I don't think Shannon will last much longer this evening. She's behaved well, but is now back to flying around on her scooter. It amuses me that the managers have to smile as they are forced by this tornado of an 8-year-old child to jump out of the way.

'We can get an something from the ice cream van outside on the way to the car, if you like?'

She does like.

Lily sees me and asks if we can go now.

I nod. 'But first there's someone I think you might like to see.'

She raises a quizzical eyebrow.

'Marilyn is here.'

She gasps. 'Where? Where?'

I lead her to the table by the fire doors and watch the girls chat. They give nothing away, and both play it down. Lots of teenage cool, even though Lily's reaction told me how excited she was. After a few moments I walk up to Marilyn myself and say my goodbyes. I also thank Kirsty for approaching me and explain how seeing Marilyn has made my day. I'd like to invite her over for tea but decide not to – I would have to run it by Alison and her managers and the residential home. By that the time we'd all be old.

I give Marilyn another hug. 'Bye bye, darling girl.'

My little posse is more than ready for ice cream. We wait in the queue and I decide to get a Flake 99. Shannon opts for the bright blue one that makes your tongue turn the same colour. Lily takes ages to decide, then chooses one with extra flakes. We walk slowly towards the car park, silenced by slurping.

As we reach the car, I hear, 'Louise!'

I turn around and it's Marylin. She runs up to me. 'I just wanted to say that I'm really sorry for all that I did. I loved living with you and Lloyd and Jackson and Vincent and Lily.' She barely stops for breath. 'How are Jackson and Vincent?'

I'm taken aback and my eyes fill with tears. I blink them back. 'Marilyn, all that happened back then was not your fault. I only know some of it but I know that it was not your fault at all.'

She starts to cry, and comes in for another hug.

'How's your mum?' I ask.

'She's alright. I see her every week. She's moved to the area and is trying to sort herself out so I can live with her again.'

I smile. 'That's wonderful.'

Marilyn says. 'She broke up with Alan. He's still in Yorkshire, the sad twat.'

'That's good, isn't it? I think your mum was struggling.'

Kirsty walks up to us. I smile, reach in my bag for a business card and hand it over. 'Just in case we can see Marilyn again.'

One last hug. Marilyn stands next to Kirsty, who has her arm around her. I feel full to the brim with emotion as I reverse out of my parking space and wave to them. Lily has wound down the window and is waving. Shannon is waving too, even though she hasn't the faintest idea who Marilyn is. I can see her eager blue face in the mirror.

As we drive off, Marilyn runs after us for a few steps, still waving and smiling.

Now the tears come.

Afterword

For decades the metaphor of climbing a corporate ladder was used to infer starting one's career at the bottom and taking steps toward the top. The climb was expected to be progressive, challenging and rewarding.

As foster carers we work for the corporate parent where the ladder means something very different. Our ladder is often old and shaky, we carry a heavy load as we climb up to the unknown, and the wall that the ladder is leaning against keeps moving. The people who said that they would stand at the bottom and hold the ladder to keep us safe walked off. We're not even sure why we are climbing the ladder since there is nothing for us at the top. We do it because we are asked to, because it is expected of us. It's treacherous and can be lonely. And if we fall off, we are made to feel that it was our fault.

Career ladders do not apply to foster carers, if we are honest a career does not exist. We are seen as nannies, babysitters, parking bays, pot washers ffor traumatised children and young people. How that happens is not cut and dried and not always the families' fault. Life happens.

Those of you who foster and read my books will recognise my stories from your own experiences. The birth parents and families who read my books will also recognise themselves, some of you tell me so. It's different with the professionals. Some will nod and say 'yep this happens', many will want to brush mine and other stories under the carpet. But I beg you to stop this, those old social work theories about children and attachment need to be refreshed. Many of the texts the professionals read as students were written by predominantly white, middle aged, middle class privileged men over 70 years ago.

The scholars of children's social care who are not recognised or taken seriously are the people who were in care themselves, who were neglected and abused and experienced trauma. I am still shocked and saddened by professionals' attitudes towards those who have experienced the care system from within it, who survived it and have got the best ideas on how to improve it. I beg you to take us seriously, I beg you to stop feeling threatened by us, to stop dismissing us by describing us as 'angry'. Of course we're angry and that's where the answers lie to improve this broken, degrading system.

I would also beg you to treat foster carers well – no foster carers, no fostering! My professional colleagues, how would you feel if people without your experience or qualification kept telling you how to do your job? I'm pretty sure that you would get fed up. So, a hairdresser who cuts and styles hair every day and has customers and runs the salon, and has done for years, has to sit down with the aromatherapist, so that the aromatherapist can tell the hairdresser where they are going wrong. Why? We are in a crisis, nationally and internationally, when we fail to identify as 'nations who look after our children'. Because if we do not, then who *are* we?

Marilyn, like most children who come into care, did so under what is known as a 'Section 20'. Under Section 20 of the Children Act 1989, a child or young person may be accommodated by the local authority where there is agreement to this arrangement by those with parental responsibility. The child becomes looked after by someone else in this arrangement. Sometimes, well if I'm honest, often, when I have tried to work with birth mums, it has been tricky. I completely understand why. The child is in care because of a number of reasons, but mostly it boils down to the reality that the parent could not meet their needs. Put like that, it sounds like it was about food and money and accommodation. More often, it's also about abuse and neglect.

Marilyn's mum did not abuse her child – at least not intentionally, and not in a way that might be obviously seen as abuse. It was far more complicated than that. Emily was herself in an abusive relationship with her partner and, like so many women, economically challenged as a result. How many women are forced to make choices just to have a roof over their and their children's heads? Marilyn became involved with bad people, as so many children do when they are not under the wing of a watchful adult. Emily never wanted her daughter to go and live with her own parents. She knew how difficult it would be for a child like Marilyn to live according to their strict religious code. I don't know whether Emily suffered sexual abuse at the hands of her father. Robert was never prosecuted. The accusation of sexual abuse against Marilyn was lost in the larger County Lines case.

These days, Marilyn lives with her mother almost all the time. Emily has been amazing, although we had our uncomfortable moments. At times, when Marilyn was living with us, I felt Emily try to would undermine me. When I shared information about Marilyn's behaviour, Emily would text or call Marilyn and tell her what I had said. We are on good terms now, although it took a while.

When you are the foster carer it is your job to parent. When you have had your child taken away from you, you are playing a different role. Emily wanted to atone for the past and be seen as the rescuer, the saviour, the good mum. In reality, Emily still had some maturing to do herself, because of what had happened to her. That's why I say that it is difficult to know where anyone's story 'begins'. I don't blame Emily. Instead, I try to put myself in her position. What would I do if my child was being looked after by someone else? I would hate it, that's for sure.

After Marilyn left, other pieces of the jigsaw slotted together a little bit more. We could not fathom the actions of Fearsome Freda in her olive-green uniform. I'm still reeling from the fact that she did what she did. Somehow, someone gave her permission. I don't know if it was a manager or the universe, but she felt entitled to make us pay for her idea to 'save' Marilyn. We never did get the money back, just a little amusement watching various administrative departments at Social Services avoid the conversation. Moira went down several notches in my estimation. The fact that she and her fellow social workers would not respond when I talked about County Lines ultimately put a child in danger – not to mention sending my stress levels through the roof.

Here is what I think was really going on and why this story is different. Over the years that I have been fostering it is easy to see how fragile this sector has become. It is simply too hard to manage the needs of the children when those needs are so great and resources so limited. The children are usually at the back of the line when it comes to decision-making. Freda was a good friend of Moira's manager. That might be considered a conflict of interest, but it's nothing new in this sector. I suspect Freda was used to having her own way, given what a forceful woman she was. I also suspect that the manager and others were quite glad to see the back of her, though they would never say so. I suspect poor Moira felt that she had to do what she did. She was expected to follow Freda's lead, regardless of what she believed. We ended up paying the price for power politics and personality clashes.

Then there was the County Lines issue. Since Theresa May slashed police budgets and policing in 2015 we have had 22,000 fewer officers on the ground. We have seen the closure of over 600 police stations. Organised crime is able to flourish. And County Lines is thriving. Drug dealers in major cities establish networks for the supply and sale of drugs to users in towns and rural areas by using other people (typically those who are young or otherwise vulnerable) to carry, store and sell the drugs.

On information websites we are told that 'police are urging people to look out for the signs of County Lines drug dealing'. It's what happens after that which interests and worries me. I can notice activity but then what? To whom do I report it? And what action will then be taken? It has become harder and harder to report anything to the police. Who is picking up the slack?

The schools largely now belong to academy trusts with reputations to protect. Not only that, but their teachers and safeguarding officers are overworked and under-resourced – even if they wanted to, they just don't have the capacity to deal with the problem. The children's social care system is big and disconnected, and inefficient as a result. This is a fatal combination which results in years of unresolved serious issues such as the expansion of County Lines.

County Lines has become our new social norm. Things

that we could never imagine or don't really want to know about do actually happen.

I'm pleased that Marilyn has stayed in touch. We actually hear from her more frequently than most children. Normally it's the family or new carers who stay in touch initially, and then only for a limited time. I think keeping hold of the healthy attachments formed across the care system is something we should try harder to do. Foster carers' requests to stay in touch can become lost in the wind, and time moves on.

I felt a bond with Marilyn right from the first moments. I could see things in her that others didn't. It only takes a little bit of looking. She is bright and vivacious; she is a survivor. She has managed to stay away from the County Lines gang for now and I hope, as she gets older, the Lines will fade. Marilyn and her mother were thinking about changing her name. It is, after all, a very recognisable name for a young woman these days. How many do you know?

Weirdly, I think there were crossovers in Marilyn's story with the real life story of Marilyn Monroe. Both were misunderstood and exploited by men for the men's gain.

It's fair to say that Lloyd and I are both tired now. Not of the children; they are endlessly fascinating. They are wonderful and we love earning their trust. It has been an enormous privilege to have worked with so many over the years. *There can be no keener revelation of a society's soul than the way in which it treats its children* is an observation attributed to Nelson Mandela. I absolutely agree.

What Lloyd and I are tired of is a broken system in which there are too many people who don't know about fostering or don't care. Who knows why they are there? Perhaps the money is the lure. And I don't mean that money is the lure for foster carers themselves. (You would need to be fostering six children to begin to make any money, and how could you manage the individual needs of six modern, traumatised children? There is a crisis in recruitment with hardly any people stepping up to become foster carers.) The problem is higher up than the foster carers. People like me have been saying for years that things have to change. We have even suggested the solutions (always dismissed because we are 'only' foster carers). What it comes down to is that attitudes need to change. Overall, foster carers are treated badly, but the children are treated worse. Somehow it has become okay to allow children to bump around placements and then fall out at 16 or 18 into a wilderness of uncertainty.

It sometimes feels as if we are losing, Lloyd and I: losing our energy, our morale, our money, to help children who we may never see again. How much longer we can continue to keep on fighting the good fight, I don't know.

Something is very wrong with the care sector. I don't want a medal for working in it, I just need respect for what I do. But I am still proud to be a foster carer. More recently I have been instrumental in setting up a new campaign, #proudtobeafostercarer. We try never to give up hope that things will get better.

And, approaching it from another angle, I have managed to set up a charity, the Spark Sisterhood: Remarkable Women Empowering Girls Leaving Care. If you are interested, you can find out more at www.sparksisterhood.org. The vision of the charity is about creating a mentoring and networking chain between experienced and successful business women who have themselves been in care, and girls leaving the care system now. We aim to break negative cycles of struggle by offering friendship, guidance, mentoring and support to these girls as they leave the care system and are at their most vulnerable. Girls exactly like Marilyn. Girls who, given their life experiences to date are likely to struggle more profoundly with the start of independent living post care than their peers. They are at greater risk of social exclusion, homelessness, unemployment or involvement in crime. There is also the increased risk for girls leaving care of being groomed or exploited, as well as the increased likelihood of becoming pregnant compared to other teenage girls. We aim to offer tailor-made apprenticeships, funds, life skills support, job opportunities, business start-up opportunities, education and training. We also provide advice and guidance on keeping safe, while celebrating all that is important and joyful about being a woman in the 21st century.

Louise Allen, November 2023

Acknowledgements

I wouldn't be able to do what I do without the Allen team of Lloyd, Jackson, Vincent, Lily, and our hardworking (and somewhat spoilt) pooches Douglas and Dotty.

Thank you to Theresa Gooda who is me with every book. We are too far away from each other to pop in for coffee; that's probably a good thing or the work would never get done.

I would also like to thank our wonderful readers, Catherine Lloyd, Alexandra Plowman and Karen Furse, who see the first messy manuscript. They have been with us for the whole Thrown Away Children journey, and their skills and insights are invaluable.

To Jane Graham Maw, my special agent who never fails me. To my editor, Jo Sollis who makes suggestions with such kindness. And to Mirror Books collectively – you are a brilliant team.

THROWN AWAY **CHILDREN**: COMING SOON TO THE SERIES

WILLOW'S STORY
Louise Allen
with Theresa McEvoy

When Willow arrives in the Allen household, curious things begin to happen.

Who is the strange child dressed in outlandish clothes who refuses a mobile phone? What are the mysterious allegations that have been made about her?

Determined to find out Louise gets more than she bargained for, uncovering some distressing secrets as she unravels the truth about Willow's family background.

THROWN AWAY **CHILDREN:**
OTHER BOOKS IN THIS SERIES

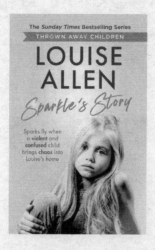

SPARKLE'S STORY
Louise Allen
with Theresa McEvoy

Louise gets a frantic call to take in a damaged and destructive young girl. Separated from her siblings Sparkle is hostile and angry.

A short while after settling in Sparkle begins to identify as pansexual. A revolution is underway in the Allen household, with Sparkle's transition motivating all of the young people to explore what becoming an adult means for them and the language and communication between everyone is in uproar.

But it's Sparkle's escalating behaviour that causes concern.

THROWN AWAY **CHILDREN:**
OTHER BOOKS IN THIS SERIES

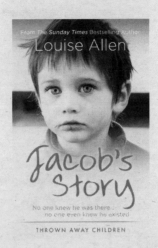

JACOB'S STORY
Louise Allen
with Theresa McEvoy

Officers from the RSPCA investigate reports of animal cruelty and neglect on a farm, only to discover a 5-year-old boy curled up asleep in a dog bed, amidst filth and squalor.

When he arrives in the Allen household, a terrified Louise wonders how on earth she will cope looking after a child with his level of physical and emotional damage. With the support of veteran social worker, Mary, the fight begins to get Jacob the support he needs – as medical investigations begin to reveal more shocking details about Jacob's story.

THROWN AWAY CHILDREN: OTHER BOOKS IN THIS SERIES

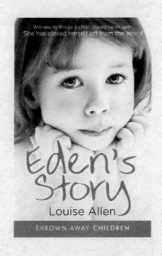

EDEN'S STORY
Louise Allen
with Theresa McEvoy

Ashley is a young single mum who governs her life by astrology and online clairvoyants. One night, unable to find a sitter for her baby daughter, Eden, she leaves her home alone, asleep... locked inside a wardrobe.

When Eden arrives at foster carer Louise Allen's home, she is five years old, she does not speak and her mother is in prison.

When she begins exhibiting other disturbing behaviour, including torturing the family pets she loves, it leads Louise to discover the pain and tragic reality behind little Eden's Story